Praise for *How to Lead Teachers to Become Great*

"I speak to thousands of teachers every year and reinforce that it is what the teacher knows and can do that is the most important factor in student achievement. Janet and Robin capture this very significant point as they provide some essential tactics for school leaders to follow so that teachers can teach and students can learn."

— Dr. Harry Wong, Author of the bestselling book in education, *The First Days of School*

"Teaching is the final common pathway of efforts to improve student achievement. Leaders who want to help teachers improve instruction will find Janet Pilcher and Robin Largue have provided a rich menu of intuitively appealing ideas and practices. What the authors offer is grounded on their extensive professional experiences and connected to solid scholarship. Those aspiring to be an 'instructional leader' will benefit from this book."

— Ronald Gallimore, Distinguished Professor Emeritus, UCLA; Coauthor of *You Haven't Taught Until They Have Learned*

"As I travel the country assessing organizations and coaching leaders, I've seen that the best businesses are those that standardize their best practices. Janet Pilcher and Robin Largue prove that the same can be true of our nation's schools. This outstanding book shows school leaders and teachers how to harvest and standardize proven best practices that improve student learning and increase parent satisfaction. By incorporating its lessons into America's classrooms, we can accomplish things that no amount of funding could ever match—successful, dedicated students, happy parents, and consistently great learning environments!"

— Quint Studer, CEO and founder of Studer Group®; Bestselling author of *Results That Last* and *Hardwiring Excellence*

"As a parenting expert, I want all children to get a superb education. Yet as a former teacher, I know the kinds of challenges educators face. And I know that our worsening economy is forcing them to do more in their classrooms with less and less. It has never been more important for school leaders to give their teachers the support they need and deserve—and this important new book provides a blueprint for making that happen. If you want better schools, better teachers, and more successful students, heed the advice in *How to Lead Teachers to Become Great*. (And I say that not just as a parenting expert and a former teacher, but also as a mom!)"

— Michele Borba, Ed.D., Educator and award-winning author of 21 books including *The Big Book of Parenting Solutions* and *Building Moral Intelligence*

"Janet and Robin passionately believe that all of our nation's students deserve the best possible teachers. Their dedication to working toward that goal shows on every page of this wonderful book. In it, they provide research-based tactics that blend business, healthcare, and education findings that focus on consistently harvesting meaningful results. *How to Lead Teachers to Become Great* will surely expand our conversations on school effectiveness and accountability. Better yet, it will help our nation's teachers to become the best they can be— and our nation's students to do the same."

— Christopher Gergen, Founding partner of New Mountain Ventures; Director of the Entrepreneurial Leadership Initiative, Duke University; Coauthor of *Life Entrepreneurs*

How to Lead Teachers to Become Great

It's All About Student Learning

Janet Pilcher and **Robin Largue**

This book is dedicated to all the students we have taught along the way —and who, in turn, have taught us so very much.

Published by:
Fire Starter Publishing
913 Gulf Breeze Parkway, Suite 6
Gulf Breeze, FL 32561
Phone: 850-934-1099
Fax: 850-934-1384
www.firestarterpublishing.com

ISBN: 978-0-9840794-3-8

Library of Congress Control Number: 2009932802

Printed in the United States of America

TABLE OF CONTENTS

The coauthors of *How to Lead Teachers to Become Great: It's All About Student Learning* believe education is all about school leaders and teachers providing a great service to students and their parents. Janet Pilcher and Robin Largue wrote this book with the belief that schools are about providing students with a great place to learn, teachers with a great place to teach, and parents with confidence that their children are getting a great education.

Both Janet and Robin have spent their professional lives as teachers and leaders. (They began their educational careers as, respectively, a high school mathematics teacher and a high school history teacher.) Today, they teach other teachers and leaders how to get the best student learning results and create results-oriented school cultures.

After 15 years of teaching, Robin became the second female to lead a high school in the Escambia County School District, Florida. After serving as the Director of Secondary Education of the Escambia County School District, she retired in 2000 to take an educational leadership faculty position at the University of West Florida (UWF). While there, she led the development and design of an online, educational leadership program that included a core of courses in the College of Business and specialization courses in educational leadership.

In the early '90s, after four years of teaching high school math students, Janet completed her doctoral degree in measurement and evaluation at Florida State University. This program ranks as one of the best programs of its kind in the country. Janet's dissertation study extended the original work of Rick Stiggins' research on grading practices. In her work with teachers and school leaders, Janet continuously incorporates the lessons she has learned from Stiggins' and his colleagues' decades of research.

Janet began her higher education career at UWF. Within her first two years at the university, the dean of the College of Education at the time asked Janet to become the associate dean of the college. She would go on to work with the school's faculty to complete the process for receiving approval of the first doctoral program at the university.

She served as the associate dean of the college for seven years until she was selected to become the dean of an expanded College of Professional Studies, which included social services, health services, and education programs. During her tenure at UWF, Janet has received over $16 million of grants and contracts used to develop and implement innovative teacher and leader professional development tools and programs.

At the beginning of 2005, Janet and Robin initiated the Institute for Innovative Community Learning (ICL), an entrepreneurial center at UWF. Their goal was to prepare and develop great teachers in today's classrooms. Over the past four years, they have had tremendous success.

The source of their success is TeacherReady® (www.teacherready.net), a one-of-a-kind online alternative pathway for certifying teachers, which leads to Florida professional certification. The program targets individuals who want to transition out of their current careers into teaching. The program is state of Florida approved and is part of the professional education unit accredited by the National Council for Accreditation of Teacher Education (NCATE).

Teachers who complete the program can work with their respective states and organizations to transfer the Florida teaching license they receive at the end of the program allowing them to teach in states other than Florida. Others living outside of Florida gain their Florida license and move to Florida to teach. Since its inception, the program has tripled in growth each year. Currently, TeacherReady students live in 16 states and 7 countries.

Janet worked with a team of researchers to develop the Lesson Architect® (lessonarchitect.uwf.edu), a free online professional development tool that helps teachers design standards-aligned lessons. Janet and Robin wrote a guide, *Aligning Instruction to Standards: Just Ask Andie*, to complement the free online tool. Currently, over 30,000 educators have accessed and now use the tool.

Two years ago, Janet and Robin connected with Dr. Harry Wong to integrate his work, which he describes in *The First Days of School: How to Be an Effective Teacher*, into TeacherReady and their other professional development resources for new teachers (www.teacherready.net). Robin also worked with Harry and Rosemary Wong to develop an online course that integrates a multimedia package developed by Harry Wong Publications, Inc.

How to Lead Teachers to Become Great is most influenced by Quint Studer. For those who don't know him, he is the founder of Studer Group®, an outcomes firm that implements evidence-based leadership systems that help clients attain and sustain outstanding results. Studer has gained national recognition as a change agent and thought leader in healthcare, linking a sustained focus on service, quality, employee, and patient satisfaction with growth and bottom-line results.

He was named one of the "Top 100 Most Powerful People in Healthcare" by *Modern Healthcare* magazine for his work on institutional healthcare improvement. He was also named "Master of Business" by *Inc.* magazine. He has helped hundreds of hospitals and healthcare systems—including recipients of the prestigious Malcolm Baldrige National Quality Award—become world-class leaders in service and operational excellence.

Studer is the author of several books, including *Hardwiring Excellence* (which has sold more than 300,000 copies since it was published in 2004) and *Results That Last* (which became an Amazon.com bestseller even before it was published in 2007 and went on to become a *Wall Street Journal* bestseller). Strategies and tactics described in both books heavily influence the ideas that appear in this one.

Interestingly, Studer started his career as a special education teacher in Janesville, Wisconsin. He spent 10 years as a teacher and leader of special education. When people ask him how his tactics in healthcare translate into education, he says, "very easily." He reports that he took what he learned from being a special education teacher and created strategies that he used to move some of the lowest performing hospitals in the country to high performing ones.

Believing that the results Studer received in healthcare and other sectors of the business world could translate directly into teachers' classrooms, Janet and Robin worked with 20 teachers and their leaders in some of the highest need schools in Pensacola, Florida, to pilot the tactics described in this book. Then, something remarkable happened. The teachers became energized, repurposed, and gained a renewed belief that they were doing worthwhile work that was making a difference in their students' and their students' parents' lives. Proof of that worthwhile work came at the end of their first 30 days when the teachers achieved improved student learning and parent satisfaction results (see Appendix 2).

After this initial ad hoc program, 100 percent of the teachers gave the highest rating, a 5 on a 5-point scale, to the survey item that asked if the teachers would recommend the professional development they received to other teachers. These positive results inspired the teachers to keep going. They had a renewed focus on implementing day-to-day practices that improved student learning and wanted to ensure their students' parents were satisfied with the education their children were provided.

Through the coauthors' lifetime work with pre-service, early career, and veteran teachers, they've found that to be great, teachers must enter their classrooms believing every student wants to learn and that they can successfully coach each student to hit one learning target at a time.

Over time the authors have created a research-based framework that teaches school leaders and teachers how to become great. The framework, which is heavily influenced by the research of Stiggins, Wong, and Studer, helps school leaders and teachers create results-oriented learning environments at their schools.

The authors gain constant inspiration from the work of Stiggins, Wong, and Studer and their commitment to providing our educational communities with tried and true best practices and evidence that those practices achieve improved student results. The authors have taken from each of these great minds to build their own successful program. From Stiggins the authors learned that when leaders and teachers use sound classroom assessment practices as a way to engage students in the learning process, students achieve at higher levels. From Harry and Rosemary Wong's book, *The First Days of School*, they learned that important progress can be made when teachers use certain best practices to manage their classrooms on the first days of school.

Through Studer's work with teachers, school leaders, nurses, doctors, and CEOs and Stiggins' and Wong's work with educators all over the world, the trio have helped make a difference in the lives of others.

In this book, the coauthors outline the tactics they've created based on the great work of these educators and others mentioned in Appendix 1, who have each contributed to the research base for the "what," "why," and "how" of the authors' tactics.

The authors created the tactics with the goal of helping school leaders and teachers achieve improved student learning. In this book they show confirmed results that the tactics can do exactly that. Read on to learn more about evidence-based classroom learning and the tactics that can be implemented in order to achieve it.

Evidence-Based Classroom Learning

Great school leaders recognize that teachers are what make great schools. They know that their teachers are the number one influencing factor affecting student learning, and consequently, parent satisfaction. In short, great teachers are those who achieve student learning goals during the school year and thus create satisfied students and parents.

How to Lead Teachers to Become Great includes a description of 14 tactics school leaders must implement in order to recruit, retain, coach, and support effective teaching in their schools. In addition, this book guides teachers on what they can expect from school leaders as they continue to develop each day to become better and better at what they do.

Each chapter provides a description of the tactic being covered, information regarding the relevance of each tactic, and an overview on how the tactic must be applied. The first four tactics focus on what leaders must do to recruit and retain high performing teachers. The remaining ten tactics describe what teachers need to know and apply to produce improved student learning and parent satisfaction results. These latter tactics also help school leaders know how to coach and support teachers to become great. The 14 tactics represent the actions that school leaders must take to staff a school of great teachers and that teachers must take to ensure they are providing the education their students deserve.

The results these tactics can yield are undeniable. Through teacher satisfaction survey results, we have learned that teachers who learn and apply these

14 tactics become more satisfied with their work and gain a renewed belief that they are making a difference in the lives of their students.

Jim Collins begins his best-selling book, *Good to Great*, stating, "Good is the enemy of great." He specifically suggests that most people perceive schools to be good, but few judge them as great. We contend that great teachers make great schools and that most teachers have a strong desire to make a difference in the lives of their students. It's dedicated support from school leaders, who refuse to settle for a "good" school or "good" teachers, that can help good teachers become great.

To create school environments where students want to learn and are inspired to achieve, we suggest school leaders first recognize that the teacher is the most important variable affecting student learning. Robert Marzano's research reinforces this belief.

In 2003, Marzano and a team of researchers analyzed the results of several studies and found that a student scoring at the 50th percentile, who spends two years in an average teacher's classroom and in an average school, is likely to continue scoring at the 50th percentile. However, they found when that same student spends two years in a highly effective school with a highly effective teacher, his score will likely reach the 96th percentile. Conversely, when this same student spends two years in a low performing school with a poor quality teacher, his score drastically decreases to the 3rd percentile.

Some propose home environments have a greater impact on student learning than schools and teachers. For example, they suggest that if students do not receive proper support at home, they'll struggle to reach their potential, despite the efforts of dedicated teachers. Catherine Snow led a group of researchers to study the effect of home support on literacy achievement and found this belief not to be the case. In fact, the results provided further evidence of just how significant a teacher's role is in the success of her students.

Snow and her researchers found that when students had high home support, student achievement levels were jeopardized when students were in classrooms that provided little support to students. Likewise, they discovered that students reached high achievement levels when they had high classroom support even when students lived in a home with little support.

Despite the research indicating that it's teachers, not products or special curricula, that lead to great student results, we continue to see publishing and consulting companies promoting high dollar, silver bullet-type products, programs, curricula, and assessments. They emptily promise school districts and teachers miracle results in their classrooms. Sometimes these products lead to learning gains. Sometimes they don't. Usually, schools experience initial gains with little evidence that those gains will be sustained over time. The overall result is that schools and districts find few, if any, returns on their financial investments.

Unfortunately, rather than draw their focus back to supporting their teachers, the districts and school leaders too often set their sights on the next new fad and continue to practice in ways that provide little to no benefit to their students. After almost a decade of working with school leaders and teachers to build great learning environments for students, we know that many of them, despite their best efforts, struggle to achieve their required student results on a yearly basis.

The Rand Corporation sponsored the research outlined in the report, *Strong States, Weak Schools: The Benefits and Dilemmas of Centralized Accountability*. The report alleges that district and school accountability are disconnected from what occurs in their teachers' classrooms. The findings from the study, which was conducted in California, Georgia, and Pennsylvania, suggest that teachers' classrooms are relatively autonomous, and that superintendents and school leaders have only a limited influence on teacher practices.

We assert that some kind of uniformity of teacher practices is needed in classrooms. Unfortunately to date, the solutions that have been proposed by the nation's policymakers have not produced desirable results. We suggest policymakers and school leaders consider new approaches such as the one outlined in this book.

We recommend that leaders implement uniform teacher hiring practices and recruitment and teaching practices. Our 14 tactics will help them do just that. We've found that when these 14 tactics are implemented properly, teachers are able to provide their students with every opportunity to want to learn and to achieve learning gains.

The standardization we recommend does not take away a teacher's creativity nor does it mean students will be forced to learn in the same way. Rather, our tactics allow teachers more time to create and integrate creativity in their classrooms and to pay attention to the specific needs of every student. The tactics build a uniform framework for classrooms that allows teachers to focus on student learning.

It's important to make a distinction between our definition of a tactic and a goal. A tactic is different from a goal. A goal represents the outcome individuals want to achieve and has a measure attached to it to determine if, when, and how well an organization meets it. A tactic is a course of action that individuals in an organization take to help achieve the goal. The tactics presented in this book all focus on achieving two measurable goals: 1) Improve student learning, and 2) Increase parent satisfaction.

We label this framework of tactics *evidence-based classroom learning*. It combines clinical expertise and experience from professional practices, which have resulted in improving human performance in organizations throughout the country.

As previously mentioned, we borrow our framework from Quint Studer's work and results from practicing evidence-based leadership with CEOs in hospitals in the United States. Under Studer's leadership, Studer Group® has helped some of the lowest performing healthcare organizations become the highest performing in the country. In particular, healthcare organizations using what Studer calls "must haves" dramatically improved their performance in patient care, patient satisfaction, and employee satisfaction and reduced employee turnover and operational costs.

Remember, great teaching is determined by student learning and parent satisfaction results. Therefore, we designed the 14 tactics by connecting the principles associated with the "must haves" and the decades of research on effective teaching strategies.

Each year we apply the 14 tactics with school leaders and teachers working in high need schools. We have had documented success.

For example, last year we worked with 20 elementary teachers and their school leaders employed in four of the highest need schools in the Escambia County School District in Florida. The participating teachers were within their first three years of teaching or were new to teaching in high need schools. The 20 teachers showed important results in three areas—student learning, parent satisfaction, and teacher satisfaction. A summary of the results are provided in Appendix 2.

Ms. Gamble, one of the fifth grade teachers at Warrington Elementary School in Pensacola, Florida, who participated in the program, established a 30-day literacy goal focused on fluency. Students were expected to demonstrate improved fluency by 10 additional words with each reading passage. After Ms.

Gamble implemented the learning targets, activities, and assessments in her 30-day plan, her students each exceeded the 30-day goal by 10 words.

Ms. Flaherty, another fifth grade teacher participating in our program, rounded on students. Rounding is a term we borrow from physicians who do daily rounding with their patients. During her conversations with students, they identified and communicated to her what they saw as being learning barriers within the classroom. She made modifications to remove the barriers. Like Ms. Gamble, her students achieved the 30-day fluency goal.

We know that most teachers have one common purpose—they want to make a difference in the lives of those they teach each day. In this book, we show how they can ensure that goal becomes a reality. Using what we've learned from Studer Group's work with doctors, nurses, and hospitals, we teach school leaders and teachers how to improve student and teacher performance and create a framework for evidence-based classroom learning.

Please understand: Evidence-based classroom learning is not a program or product; rather it is a framework with tactics school leaders use to train and support teachers to get student learning results that last. Tactics described in this book fall within five principles of the evidence-based classroom learning framework.

Principle 1: When Teachers Know What to Expect, They Perform
Principle 2: What Teachers Permit in Their Classrooms, They Promote
Principle 3: What Teachers Measure, Students Value
Principle 4: When Teachers Coach, Students Learn
Principle 5: When Teachers Share Results, Everybody Wins

Within the book we describe each principle and associated tactics that school leaders must use to recruit, retain, coach, and support teachers to help students achieve student learning results and ensure parents that their child is receiving an outstanding learning experience.

First, school leaders must apply the first four tactics, which enable them to recruit and retain high performing teachers. Naturally, school leaders must know what great teaching looks like in order to help their teachers, new and old, become great at what they do. Next, Tactics 5-14 teach school leaders how to coach and support teachers to get student learning and parent satisfaction results.

Principles and Tactics	
Principle 1: When Teachers Know What to Expect, They Perform	
Tactic 1	Hold High, Middle, and Low Performer Conversations with Teachers
Tactic 2	Use Peer Interviewing to Help Select New Hires
Tactic 3	Hold 30- and 90-Day Meetings with New Hires
Tactic 4	Round for Outcomes on Teachers
Principle 2: What Teachers Permit in Their Classrooms, They Promote	
Tactic 5	Coach Teachers on How to Maximize Parent-Teacher Interactions
Tactic 6	Coach and Support Teachers as They Apply Classroom Rules and Procedures
Principle 3: What Teachers Measure, Students Value	
Tactic 7	Help Teachers Create and Reach Measurable Learning Targets
Tactic 8	Help Teachers Create and Follow 30-Day Plans
Tactic 9	Coach Teachers on How to Appropriately Assign Grades
Principle 4: When Teachers Coach, Students Learn	
Tactic 10	Coach and Support Teachers as They Give Specific Feedback on Learning
Tactic 11	Coach and Support Teachers as They Round for Outcomes on Students
Tactic 12	Help Teachers Harvest Student Wins
Principle 5: When Teachers Share Results, Everybody Wins	
Tactic 13	Help Teachers Successfully Roll Out Data
Tactic 14	Help Teachers Use Data to Reflect Student Progress

© Studer Group, LLC

When school leaders implement what they have learned from these tactics and recruit, retain, coach, and support teachers, teachers and students win. Teachers have a better understanding of what each of their students' "what" is—meaning what it takes for him or her to become a successful learner—and students have an increased desire to learn.

Keeping this evidence in mind, school leaders must make recruitment, selection, and development of teachers their number one priority. This book provides leaders with tactics to help them do just that while gaining higher student learning and improved parent satisfaction results.

Principle 1:
When Teachers Know What to Expect, They Perform

As leaders, we see teachers coming to work each day to make a positive difference in the lives of their students. To do that job well, they know they have to continuously learn and re-learn things that make them great teachers. Too often, however, they start the school year eager to teach and learn, only to lose momentum, become fatigued, get frustrated, and go into survival mode as the year progresses. Tragically, brand new teachers sometimes decide to quit the profession.

Principle 1 focuses on helping teachers keep their beginning of the school year momentum going in a positive direction. Principle 1 consists of four essential tactics that leaders need to implement in order to recruit and select great teachers to work in their schools:

Tactic 1: Hold High, Middle, and Low Performer Conversations with Teachers
Tactic 2: Use Peer Interviewing to Help Select New Hires
Tactic 3: Hold 30- and 90-Day Meetings with New Hires
Tactic 4: Round for Outcomes on Teachers

As previously mentioned, we borrow these strategies from Studer Group. They represent the core elements for providing a support-focused environment where teachers can continuously learn, apply, and achieve so that students in their classrooms are learning.

These four tactics will be covered in Chapters 1 through 4. Chapter 1 recommends that school leaders identify their high, middle, and low performing teachers and then do what they can to bring their low performing teachers up to standard. Chapter 2 teaches leaders how to create and implement a peer interviewing process that involves teachers in the hiring process and lets teachers know what is expected of individuals hired to teach with them.

Chapters 3 and 4 show school leaders that once they've hired a teacher, they should continue to communicate with the new hire to make sure she has the tools and equipment to do her job and to address any issues she encounters. We suggest that teachers are more likely to become higher performers when they know what the school leaders expect of them.

On pages 27 to 29 in *Results That Last*, Studer describes five critical elements employees look for from their managers. His experiences and results with healthcare organizations can help school leaders know what teachers expect of them. To get results from teachers, school leaders should apply these five critical elements:

1. School leaders care about and value their teachers.
2. Teachers have the tools and equipment needed to practice the tactics.
3. School leaders give teachers opportunities to learn and/or re-learn the tactics.
4. School leaders recognize and reward teachers for their good work.
5. School leaders deal with low performing teachers and stop hiring more of them.

The bottom line? Where these critical elements are implemented and our 14 tactics are followed, leaders create a school culture where low performers simply cannot survive. Teachers who fail to perform are forced to face consequences for that choice. And ultimately, low performers, who can be so damaging to students and other teachers, will either improve, quit, or be removed from classrooms.

Why use this framework? Because Studer has found that over 90 percent of employees perform when they know what their leader expects from them and when the leader practices the five critical actions employees want from their leaders.

The four tactics presented in Chapters 1 through 4 help leaders fulfill these workplace desires and, consequently, get better results. For schools, that means students are learning and parents are satisfied with their children's learning experience.

1

Tactic 1:
Hold High, Middle, and Low Performer Conversations with Teachers

Why Tactic 1 Is Important

One important lesson we've taken from Studer Group's® research of healthcare organizations is that moving low performers up or out of an organization heavily influences whether it can move from bad to good, good to great, or sustain greatness. In fact, Quint Studer himself deemed this realization so important that he covered it in the first chapter of his book *Results That Last*, which examines how to deal with high, middle, and low performers. (It should be noted that in his bestselling book, *Good to Great*, Jim Collins also stresses the importance of dealing with low performers. He does so in his chapter about getting the right people on the bus and the wrong ones off.)

We hear leaders constantly saying that their job is to get everyone on board with the company's organizational goals. But for many of them, it's just lip service. Studer Group has uncovered the truth, and it may be surprising to some. Their research shows evidence that it is actually impossible to get every single person within an organization on board.

The same holds true for learning institutions seeking to improve performance. School leaders simply cannot expect to get every single one of their teachers on board. That's why they must learn to properly deal with low performers. As we alluded to earlier, Marzano's research has shown the detrimental effect a low performing teacher can have on student learning. Schools cannot afford to have low performing teachers in classrooms.

Let's take a look at Studer Group's findings regarding measuring performance within organizations. The good news is that about 92 percent of employees in the typical organization *do* want to be on board. Other good news is that 34 percent of people in an organization are high performers, while 58 percent are middle performers who desire to improve their performance. The bad news is that leaders must spend the majority of their time on the 8 percent who are low performers.

Research also shows that when the low performing 8 percent are confronted about their behavior, one-third of them choose to change their performance and one-third choose to leave the organization. The remaining one-third choose to stay in the organization until the leader follows the process for removing them when they, inevitably, continue to underperform.

The bottom line? To provide teachers with a great place to work and students with a great place to learn, school leaders must learn how to deal with their low performers. Naturally, this process takes time and hard work that includes well-defined and consistent practices. But it's well worth the effort. High and middle performing teachers deserve leaders who have time to address their needs rather than leaders who are bogged down with problems caused by the low performing 8 percent. And more attentive leaders is what they'll get, if low performing teachers are managed properly.

To get the best student results, an organization should be made up of high and middle performers who are constantly learning and are constantly supported by school leaders. Throughout a teaching career, there are many ups and downs. As a result, people move in and out of middle and high performer roles. One of the key responsibilities for school leaders is to recognize when this movement has occurred with one of their teachers so that the leader can provide the support the teacher needs to help her constantly improve.

Without appropriate and meaningful professional development and training, teachers struggle to move from low to middle and middle to high performer levels. And top performers become frustrated when they want to learn but have little support from school leaders.

So, how exactly should low performers be dealt with? Let's take a look.

To begin, let us dispel a popular myth right off the bat. We hear leaders in schools and teachers preparing to be leaders in our college classes say, "You can't fire a teacher. The union protects them." Not true. Unions expect school leaders to provide specific feedback and training to help teachers improve their performance. They also expect school leaders to document poor performance if it continues after a teacher has received proper guidance and training to help her improve her performance. But in our work with local unions and through reviewing Studer Group's work with healthcare unions, we have learned that they tend to not want to protect employees who choose to continue low performer behaviors.

When school leaders look in a low performing teacher's file, they tend to see "good to very good" or sometimes "excellent" evaluations. On a 5-point scale, we see low performing teachers receiving mostly 4s and 5s. It's in these situations, when a low performer hasn't been properly evaluated by school leaders, that the union tends to protect him or her.

Within any organization—school, business, or otherwise—low performance is never a contained problem. When low performers are not dealt with properly, high and middle performing teachers find it difficult to maintain or improve their own performance levels. They deserve better. School leaders must document performance and terminate low performing teachers who fail to improve.

School leaders have a responsibility to their students as well. Low performing teachers can cause students to lose as much as two years of learning. School leaders must enumerate very specific expectations for their low performing teachers, support them with additional training, continuously monitor their performance, and encourage them to shift from being a low performing teacher to a middle performing one. (Tactics 5 through 14 guide school leaders through the type of training and support teachers need to move from low to middle and middle to high performer levels and to keep high performers excelling.)

Low performers get their energy when they successfully do two things. First, in order to recruit more naysayers, they strive to pull middle performers down to low performer levels. Second, they force high performers out. What usually happens is high performers become frustrated with leaders not dealing with low performers and eventually choose to leave to find a better school environment. Or if leaving isn't an option, they give up on being the best teachers they can be and find other avenues outside of school through which they can be high performers.

One of the few things low performers are good at is exactly that: low performance. In fact, they're masters at it. They have usually spent most of their professional lives underachieving. They are good at being low performers, and, in many instances, they outlast leaders.

One way to reduce the number of low performers at your school is not to hire more into the organization. We hear, "Sure, but I don't always have that option because I need a warm body in the classroom with kids." Low performing "warm bodies" are the wrong bodies to have in classrooms with students. By allowing low performers to stay on board, schools are neglecting students, their parents, and teachers. (For a look at the hiring practices that help schools hire middle to high performing teachers, see Chapter 2!)

How to Apply Tactic 1

Teachers expect leaders to know them, what they are good at, and what they value in an organization. The performance level of the teacher should direct the type of performance conversation a leader has with him or her. *Results That Last* provides some meaningful recommendations for holding conversations with high, middle, and low performers. It also suggests that leaders hold conversations with high performers first and low performers last to show that leaders value the high performers.

In a school setting, high performers share the school values, know how to problem solve, and serve as good mentors for other teachers. In conversations with high performers, a leader should cover where the organization is going, thank the teacher for her work, outline why the teacher is important to the school, and ask the teacher what kind of support she needs from him.

Middle performers are the backbone of the organization and usually determine a school's success or failure. Most new teachers come into our schools as middle performers in the classroom and need immediate support in order to transition into high performers. Middle performing teachers know how to identify problems and bring them to the leader's attention to be solved. They also don't mind solving problems when they are given some direction and support.

Middle performer conversations should flow in the following way: Tell the teacher that he is important to the school. Then, share ONE area for the teacher to work on to improve. The leader ends the meeting letting the teacher know she is committed to his success and asks if she can do anything to help him with the area of improvement discussed.

Low performers drain the energy out of their coworkers and leaders as they attempt to keep the organization from achieving the desired results. Low performing teachers love to recruit new and middle performing teachers into their low performing camp. Their reasoning? The more low performers there are the easier it will be for them to disguise their behaviors. And covered up bad behavior means they can last longer in the organization.

Now for the low performers. *Results That Last* describes several survival skills low performers demonstrate. First, they tend to blame others for their low performance. They point their finger at leadership for not providing them with the necessary training to do a good job. Or, they unload a personal problem with coworkers or leaders to divert attention away from their performance. Generally, everyone knows who the low performers are in an organization—everyone, that is, except for the low performers themselves.

There are two important keys to ensuring that low performer conversations lead to success. First, before beginning these conversations, leaders should lay the groundwork with their bosses so that everyone in the administration is on the same page. Second, after the initial low performer conversation with a teacher, a leader must follow up relentlessly. The teacher is counting on the lack of follow-up so that her continued low performance can go unnoticed and so that she can continue her influence on middle performing teachers.

Low performer conversations can be difficult. That's why Studer created the DESK approach. The approach provides leaders with a guide to get them through these difficult conversations and helps them cut right to the chase. And before you begin, keep in mind that conversations with low performers should never start on a positive note or with casual conversation. Instead, leaders should:

Describe what has been observed.
Evaluate how they feel.
Show what needs to be done.
Know and share the consequences of continued low performance.

Let's look at an example. Meet Ms. Heinz and Ms. Aaron. Ms. Heinz is a veteran teacher at Jackson Branch Elementary School who enters each day with an infectiously negative attitude and who likes to control leaders. In fact, she successfully controlled the former leader of the school. As a result, that leader was placed in another school and recently Ms. Aaron became the new principal at Jackson Branch. Her marching orders: Turn the school around. Pronto!

It doesn't take long before Ms. Aaron discovers that Ms. Heinz is part of the school's problem, so she schedules a meeting with her. To ensure a successful conversation, she'll use the DESK approach during the meeting. Here's how it plays out:

Ms. Heinz enters Ms. Aaron's office and Ms. Aaron asks her to take a seat. She begins:

> **D**escribe what has been observed:
> Ms. Heinz, as you know, every month I ask teachers to provide the student results from their 30-Day Plans. Last month you failed to report that information. At our last meeting, you informed me that you would do so this month. When I reviewed this month's 30-day student results reports, I noticed that you again failed to submit the information.
>
> **E**valuate how they feel:
> Ms. Heinz, as a school we analyze these results each month to make sure our students are progressing and to identify learning gaps that need to be addressed. Your failure to report the information is placing our students in jeopardy.
>
> **S**how what needs to be done:
> Next Monday I would like for us to meet after school. I will review with you the proper procedure for completing 30-Day Plans and reporting their results. I will then give you a report to complete at the end of each week. And we will meet every Monday for a month so that I am sure that you understand clearly how to complete the 30-day student reports and document their results. I expect you to turn in the weekly information and meet with me each week. I also expect you to turn in your 30-day student results reports each month.

Know and share the consequences of continued low performance: Ms. Heinz, consider this your verbal warning. If you fail to complete the steps I've laid out or you fail to turn in any of the year's remaining 30-day student results reports, you will receive a written warning. Ms. Heinz, to make sure that we have a common understanding, give me a summary of what you have heard and what is expected of you.

If Ms. Heinz is a skilled low performer, she will likely try to give Ms. Aaron excuses or even blame Ms. Aaron for her behavior. But the conversation could be just the push she needed to see the light. She may then decide to turn things around, to modify her actions and become a more valuable member of the school team.

We find that most teachers change their negative behaviors and actions when a leader confronts rather than ignores their low performer behaviors. The bottom line is that low performers must be confronted. Ignoring their negative actions will not make the issues go away. Even worse, when leaders ignore poor performance and unproductive behaviors, the school becomes a breeding ground for low performance.

As mentioned before, follow-up in this scenario will be key. One failure to follow up puts Ms. Heinz back in a position to repeat her negative behavior. If Ms. Heinz continues to perform poorly, Ms. Aaron needs to immediately address the behaviors, offer and provide support to change the behaviors, and then follow up with Ms. Heinz again.

Ms. Heinz will make one of three decisions: 1) Choose to change her behavior, 2) Leave the school, or 3) Continue with her same actions. If this behavior and others continue, it may be time for Ms. Aaron to consider termination.

Throughout this process, Ms. Aaron should also be documenting these conversations as well as Ms. Heinz's subsequent improvement or continuing low performance. She should also be working with her immediate supervisor to keep him informed of the problem. To successfully deal with low performers, upper management must be on board. Their support will be essential if indeed the time comes that a school leader recommends dismissing a low performing teacher.

Of course at any time during this process, Ms. Heinz could go to the union to file a grievance. If this happens, Ms. Aaron can present the documentation of the meetings, required actions, support and training provided, and the follow-up with Ms. Heinz.

If you're feeling overwhelmed, relax. Remember, only about 8 percent of employees in an organization are low performers, and most of them will improve or change negative behaviors to positive ones after they are addressed by a leader.

For a little inspiration, here's a story with a winning outcome: Every summer we administer teacher academies for new teachers in high need schools. In one of our academies of 30 teachers, we had three who qualified as low performers. One teacher did not think she needed to attend because she believed she already knew most everything that the others were learning. We pointed out to her that, often, low performing teachers are the ones who fail to recognize a good learning opportunity. Because we called her out on her negative behavior, she reflected on her actions. She decided to become a more reflective learner and to be more engaged with her team of teachers.

During the same academy, two other teachers sat together with seemingly little interest in learning. You could say they were there in body but not in spirit. They wanted to attend so they could check a box indicating they attended the academy and receive the resulting pay. However, one of the two teachers completed an assignment that demonstrated excellent work. We shared her great work with the group. And that simple act of recognition spurred both teachers into action. They both became more engaged and better performers.

The psychology behind the turnaround is basic. Being recognized as having done something "good" made the teacher feel worthwhile. Her teaching partner saw how feeling worthwhile helped her colleague become better. As a result, both changed their approach to learning. When all was said and done, they had both produced excellent work in the academy—great work that translated into improving their teaching practices. Most importantly, they recharged their love for teaching.

Great leaders can achieve similar results in organizations in all industries. By simply taking the proper steps to address low performers and encouraging them to change their behavior through a structured approach, great leaders can turn these "problem" employees into middle and high performers. And though it's hard work, the improved learning environment will be better for all.

Tactic 2:
Use Peer Interviewing to Help Select New Hires

Why Tactic 2 Is Important

To improve student learning, school leaders need to get the right people on the bus (so to speak!) and then do whatever they can to keep them in their classrooms. An added bonus? Hiring the right teachers puts more pressure on low performers to leave or change their behaviors.

Jim Collins and his research team discovered that great leaders know that to make an organization great, they have to begin with "who"—the employees—rather than "what"—the curriculum materials, teaching programs, and so forth.

In this chapter we describe an essential tactic for hiring teachers—peer interviewing. And then in Chapters 3 and 4 we address two essential tactics leaders must apply in order to keep teachers once they are hired.

Evidence from Studer Group's® work in healthcare indicates that leaders get better results from their employees when they use peer interviewing to help select new hires. We've found that this rule applies to school environments as well. Let's take a look at peer interviewing and how it can help you take your school to the next level.

Selecting the right teachers is one of the most important decisions school leaders make. Not only will these teachers contribute to the overall culture of the school, but they will make or break how well the school's students will learn. Once a school leader has dealt properly with low performing teachers and created a high performing school culture, he has to make a commitment to hire the right teachers who will support the new culture of excellence.

By and large, hiring practices for selecting new teachers vary by schools and school districts. Sometimes teachers are selected by school districts and placed at schools. At other times, school leaders make the selections. Regardless of how the teachers are chosen, however, one thing holds true for most schools—rarely are the teachers themselves consulted about the kind of colleagues they would like to have join the faculty.

It's time for that tradition to end. We recommend that leaders use peer interviewing when selecting teachers each year. Here's why: First, middle to high performing teachers—whom you should enlist for peer interviews—will want to hire people like them. They'll be able to easily recognize which candidates value what they value regarding education and who they think will thrive in the school's culture.

Second, the teachers will be much more willing to work with new hires when they have a little skin in the game. When they have helped choose a candidate, they want that person to succeed and are much more willing to put in the time and effort to ensure that she works each day focused on student learning and contributing to a results-oriented culture. Today, there are all kinds of ways to become a teacher. Options for teacher training include the traditional four- to five-year college or university programs and alternative pathways, such as our program TeacherReady,® which was created in 2005 for those going into teaching as their second career.

What's interesting is that the latest research shows that teacher preparation paths make little difference in determining how well a teacher's students will achieve in the classroom. The content and quality of the experiences teachers have during training are better indicators of teacher and student success. We've found that when prospective teachers successfully complete Teacher-Ready, they are able to go out and become high performing professionals.

To date, 94 percent of those who have completed the program have been hired and have become successful teachers in their respective schools. On average and across all survey items, 75 percent of the teachers coming out of our program rate their training experience at the highest level, a "5" rating.

Just as traditional training and alternative preparation programs prepare soon-to-be teachers in different ways, so does prior working experience. Many veteran teachers will come into a new school environment still entrenched in their previous school's culture and with its values in mind.

School leaders and the teacher peers who will be doing the interviews should keep in mind that it isn't the teacher's training history or work history that is important. What *is* key is her willingness to learn and implement the tactics that will lead to improved student learning and parent satisfaction results.

Some new teachers may be familiar with the tactics; others will not be. Regardless, during the interview find out whether or not the prospective hire values the results-oriented learning environment and school culture the tactics reinforce. Both types of teachers are worth hiring.

How to Apply Tactic 2

The teachers selected to be peer interviewers should include middle to high performers with at least one representative from the department or grade level of the job position. School leaders should also make sure that these teachers have a strong working knowledge of the 14 tactics covered in this book and the school culture and student learning environment the tactics help to create.

School leaders and teachers should all be on the same page regarding these tactics. The teachers should be fully aware of how the tactics contribute to the results-oriented environment the leader is trying to instill at the school. And the leader should make sure the teachers recognize the value of hiring peers who either already know or who express a desire and willingness to learn the tactics. The more teachers follow our tactics by the letter, the better chance the school will have at achieving improved student learning and greater parent satisfaction.

School leaders will get better hiring results by using peer interviewing teams to help select new hires. The school leader puts in place a process for selecting peer interview teams.

Once the peer interview team is selected, the school leader first screens the applicants and passes the ones he views as most hirable on to the peer interview team. School leaders should never submit individuals they don't want to hire. That way the leader can ensure that the interview team picks a desirable candidate. The peer interview team interviews the applicants, makes a final decision, and sends that decision to the school leader.

We recommend that the school leader follows the recommendation of the peer interview team. If the leader elects to make a different selection, he should meet with the peer interview team to provide a rationale for the decision.

We recommend that peer interview teams use the decision matrix created by Studer Group when reviewing the candidate applications and interviewing the candidates. The decision matrix consists of the desired behavior or practice, the weight of each item, and a scale for scoring the applicant. For the best results, set the decision matrix up by using prompts based on Tactics 5 to 14, which will be covered later in the book. These tactics have been developed to cover each of the desired behaviors and practices teachers at any school should value.

The decision matrix can include both performance- and behavior-based questions focused on the tactics. Performance-based questions help the interview teams determine how well a teacher can apply a particular tactic. Behavior-based questions help the interview teams determine the way the teacher values student learning and parent satisfaction.

First, decide which tactics are most important to your school. Next, create the question prompts and determine the weight of each prompt. For example, a prompt rated a 3 would be considered "Essential," a behavior a teacher must have and that is one of the most important behaviors; 2 would be "Preferred," a behavior a teacher should have; 1 would be "Helpful," a behavior that is beneficial but not necessary for a teacher to have. The weights will come into play during the scoring process.

Let's look at a performance-based prompt and a behavior-based prompt on the scoring sheet. The performance-based prompt asks a teacher to provide an example for how he would implement Tactic 7, which is described by the prompt (Figure 2.1). The behavior-based prompt asks a teacher how he values the feedback that is derived when Tactic 10 is implemented (Figure 2.2).

Figure 2.1. Performance-Based Question Sample on Tactics

Interview Prompt – Performance-Based	Weight of Item	Candidate 1 Score	Weighted Score	Candidate 2 Score	Weighted Score
Give me a literacy learning target in measurable terms that you would expect students to achieve in their first 30 days. To get students to achieve that 30-day learning target, what would you expect them to know at the end of weeks 1, 2, 3, and 4?	3 Essential 2 Preferred 1 Helpful	5 Excellent 4 Very Good 3 Fair 2 Poor 1 Very Poor		5 Excellent 4 Very Good 3 Fair 2 Poor 1 Very Poor	

© Studer Group, LLC

Figure 2.2. Behavior-Based Question Sample on Tactics

Interview Prompt – Behavior-Based	Weight of Item	Candidate 1 Score	Weighted Score	Candidate 2 Score	Weighted Score
Your principal asked you to submit evidence that students have achieved the learning goals during the first 30 days of school. Do you think this request helps improve student learning? If so, why? If not, what else could the principal ask you to do that would improve student learning?	3 Essential 2 Preferred 1 Helpful	5 Excellent 4 Very Good 3 Fair 2 Poor 1 Very Poor		5 Excellent 4 Very Good 3 Fair 2 Poor 1 Very Poor	

© Studer Group, LLC

In each figure, the individual team member scores the response for each candidate using a 1-5 scale. The interviewer then multiplies the score by the weight to get a weighted score for each candidate. When the interview is complete, each interviewer adds the weighted scores on all interview prompts to get a total score for each candidate. The scores across team members are added by candidate to achieve a final score. The interview team can then determine the candidate with the highest score.

Of course, using a peer interview approach and a decision matrix with performance- and behavior-based prompts will take longer than simply saying

"You're hired!" to the first teacher to walk through the door or to a teacher interviewed by the school leader only. Most importantly, a team approaches each interview focusing on teacher behaviors that will result in improved student learning and higher parent satisfaction. It's time well spent.

Remember, one of the most important decisions leaders and teachers make is the teachers they hire. Hiring decisions directly affect the learning gains or losses students make in a given year. The reality is that spending several hours on ensuring that the right decision is made with a new hire will be far less burdensome than the year or two it could take for a leader to remove a low performing teacher.

Selecting the right teachers and assigning them to the right places in our schools saves a lot of heartaches and prevents painful headaches for leaders, teachers, and their students.

CHAPTER

Tactic 3:
Hold 30- and 90-Day Meetings with New Hires

Why Tactic 3 Is Important

When reviewing data from healthcare organizations, Studer Group® discovered that 25 percent of the organizations' new hires left within their first 90 days. Similar to healthcare, school systems lose too many new teachers during their first semester, first year, and first three years of teaching. Too often schools successfully recruit and hire these teachers but don't do enough to retain them for the long haul. Some don't even make it through their first 90 days—the most difficult time in a new teacher's professional life. In fact, of those teachers who leave in their first three years of teaching, about *one-third* leave within the first 90 days.

Actually, the first 90 days at a new school are crucial for experienced teachers too. That's because it's during those 90 days that they must make their biggest adjustments to their new environment.

To help solve their clients' turnover problems, Studer Group implemented the 30- and 90-day meetings method for new hires. Basically, healthcare and business leaders hold 30- and 90-day meetings with new employees, allowing them to connect and build relationships with their new hires and receive valuable feedback from them. Studer Group found that when leaders had successful meetings, the new employee turnover rate was reduced by 66 percent.

Leaders holding 30- and 90-day meetings with new hires show teachers that they are committed to making the school a great place to work—a place where teachers can teach, students can learn, and parents are satisfied with their child's experience. These meetings lead to new teachers who are happier, more comfortable, and more able to focus on the most important task at hand—providing a quality education for their students. Ultimately, they create a results-oriented school environment in which student learning is maximized and parent satisfaction scores increase.

How to Apply Tactic 3

During the first 90 days of the school year, leaders schedule two one-on-one meetings with the new teachers hired—the first to be held at the 30-day mark, the second at the 90-day mark.

School leaders should make it clear to new hires that these meetings are part of "business as usual" at the school. Too often when leaders ask to meet with employees, they are sharing bad news or identifying a problem that needs to be corrected. When a school leader calls a teacher to the principal's office, teachers begin to wonder what they've done wrong. By letting teachers know up-front that these meetings will be occurring, leaders can reduce that anxiety.

In order for the meetings to be successful, Studer Group recommends that school leaders ask specific questions. There are four key questions leaders should ask new hires at the 30-day meeting, then repeat along with two additional questions at the 90-day meeting. Encourage teachers to be open and honest at these meetings. Do not accept short, non-descriptive answers. Leaders, too, should dig as deep as possible in order to engage in a meaningful conversation with teachers.

Figure 3.1 provides the 30-day questions and the two additional questions leaders ask at the 90-day meeting.

Figure 3.1. 30- and 90-Day Meeting Questions

30-Day and 90-Day Questions	
Question 1	How do we compare to what we said we would be like?
Question 2	Tell me what you like. What is going well?
Question 3	I noticed you came to us from _____. Are there things you did there that might be helpful to us?
Question 4	Is there anything here that you are uncomfortable with?
90-Day Questions Only	
Question 5	Is there anyone you know who might be a valuable addition to our team?
Question 6	As your supervisor, how can I be helpful?

© Studer Group, LLC

The 30- and 90-day meetings reinforce that school leaders are committed to retaining the teachers they and their peer interview team selected. In fact, the peer interview team's job isn't over on the new hire's first day. School leaders should relay the feedback they've heard from new hires to the peer interview team. Doing so further strengthens the stake the peer interview team feels they have in the new teacher's success. After receiving the feedback, they'll know how to better work with the new teacher in order to help her become a successful peer.

In the next section, we review Tactic 4, rounding for outcomes on teachers. This tactic provides an additional way for leaders to build relationships with teachers and to gather useful information from them that can be used to make the school a great place to work and can also help retain new teachers hired.

Ultimately, holding 30- and 90-day meetings, along with Tactic 4, rounding for outcomes on teachers, builds a supportive school culture in which problems are proactively addressed and individuals are recognized for work that produces results.

Mr. Beck's 30-Day Meeting with His Principal, Ms. Morton

Ms. Morton: Good morning, Mr. Beck. Thank you for taking time out of your schedule to meet with me today. I am interested in making sure that your first semester at Grover High School is the best that it can be for you. So, I am going to ask you a couple of questions and I would really appreciate your honest and sincere answers. I want to know how your experience is with us at Grover High so far. Mr. Beck, how do we compare to what we said we would be like when you interviewed with us?

Mr. Beck: Everything is fine. I think you are what you said you would be.

Ms. Morton: I remember saying that our actions should show that we are interested in student learning. On a scale of 1 to 10, how well are we doing?

Mr. Beck: About a 7.

Ms. Morton: What would make us a 10?

Mr. Beck: I get frustrated with too many interruptions in class. Announcements are made on the intercom through out the day. I lose my focus and so do my students. I then have a difficult time getting them back on task and focused. So, I guess reducing the interruptions could help.

Ms. Morton: Can you think of anything else?

Mr. Beck: No, not now.

Ms. Morton: Well, if you do, let me know. I will work with the teacher leadership team to do a more thorough analysis of the interruptions caused by using the public announcement system throughout the day. Thank you for calling that to my attention. Mr. Beck, tell me what is going well for you here at Grover High.

Mr. Beck: So many things. The first day of school was very organized and that has continued during the first month. Also, I find my team of teachers to be very helpful.

Ms. Morton: That is great to hear. Our teachers are committed to making Grover a great place to work and I appreciate their commitment. I noticed you came to us from Greenville High School on the north side of town. Are there things you or they did there that might be helpful to us?

Mr. Beck: Yes, the school had a "Need Supplies" bucket by the principal's office. When we were running out of supplies that were essential, we could place the need in the bucket. A teacher leader evaluated the items in the bucket each day to determine the "essential" supply needs and shared the information with the principal. That was great—I did not fear running out of essential supplies.

Ms. Morton: Thank you for sharing that idea. We value teachers having essential supplies, so that type of strategy could be very valuable for teachers at Grover High. I will share this with the teacher leadership team as well. Mr. Beck, is there anything here that you are uncomfortable with? At this point, is there anything occurring with your job here that could cause you to make a decision to leave?

Mr. Beck: Oh no. I am very happy at Grover. Thank you for asking.

Ms. Morton: Thank you, Mr. Beck, for providing open and honest answers. I want you to know that I am committed to keeping you here at Grover High School. I will get back with you on two items by the end of this week, the issue of too many announcements on the intercom system and the response from the teacher leadership team about your idea for a "Need Supplies" box. Have a good day today, Mr. Beck.

C H A P T E R

Tactic 4:
Round for Outcomes on Teachers

Why Tactic 4 Is Important

Teachers often complain that school leaders do not spend enough time in their classrooms, and as a result are unaware of what they do and what their most pressing needs are. When evaluation time arrives, a typical school leader goes into a teacher's classroom for a relatively short amount of time, assesses the teacher, usually giving high marks on the evaluation, and sends the evaluation to the teacher to review and sign.

High and middle performing teachers often tell us that they would like for their school leaders to know and care more about what is going on in their classrooms. They want their leaders to know what is important to them. They do not expect their leaders to make everyone happy all the time. But, they do expect leaders to know what teacher needs are and to care enough about them to find solutions that meet them.

High and middle performing teachers want to work in a place they enjoy and where they can prosper and learn. Most importantly, they want to work in a place that lends them every opportunity to make a difference in the lives of their students. In order for a school to meet each of these needs, its leaders must be attentive and must care about the issues teachers are facing in the classroom.

When leaders recruit great teachers, they want to keep them. Rounding, based on a technique doctors have practiced for years with their patients, can help them do just that. As part of its methodology, Studer Group® teaches its healthcare clients that it is important for staff leaders to round on their employees. The practice has been tremendously successful in helping healthcare leaders increase employee retention, among other benefits.

Many leaders say that providing them with an effective way to engage with staff is the number one item that improves staff performance. With rounding, Studer Group has created a way for leaders to gather information so that they can handle issues or needs in a proactive rather than reactive way. High performing leaders are happy to take the time to round on their employees because they know it will allow them to gather valuable information from their staff—information that when addressed will make it easier for everyone to do a great job.

Rounding is also cost effective. In its work with healthcare organizations, Studer Group has found that leaders who round on employees and employees who round on patients produce more efficient systems that yield a maximum return on investment. Rounding yields patients who are satisfied with their care and who choose to return for additional care. It also yields employees who are satisfied with their workplace and elect to stay with the organization.

How to Apply Tactic 4

Rounding can yield similar positive results in school environments. Rounding for outcomes on teachers provides school leaders with a way to establish genuine relationships with them. Many leaders get so caught up in the details of the day that they tend to forget their employees are experiencing life in different and unique ways, which bring both meaningful moments and hardships. When leaders round on their employees, they gain an opportunity to learn what is occurring in their employees' lives.

Remember, most teachers have never experienced their leaders rounding on them. Therefore, before implementing the practice, leaders need to tell their teachers what they will be doing and why. Otherwise, teachers may become fearful or suspicious of rounding and other new leadership practices.

Based on our own experiences working with schools, we provide various methods leaders can use to standardize rounding in their schools. That said, we cannot emphasize enough how important it is for leaders to commit themselves to regular rounding and to also standardize methods for processing the information received from the practice. By rounding, leaders can be proactive about solving problems and help their schools retain great teachers.

As school leaders round, they should record the information from their conversations with teachers. The information needs to be kept in a file or database so that leaders can easily access the information in order to make sure they have properly addressed any issues that arose during a teacher conversation. If a school leader cannot resolve an issue, he needs to tell the teacher that he cannot do what is wanted or requested and explain why. Remember, teachers do not always expect to get their way. But they do expect leaders to communicate answers to them.

Most of the time, leaders cannot grant requests either because of budgetary constraints or because the action requested does not align with the mission or goals of the school. But even conversations that end in denials are beneficial for the leader and the teacher. These conversations help the teacher understand more about the school, and, consequently, encourage her to become more engaged in achieving school goals. And of course, they also allow the leader to learn more about the teacher's concerns.

Remember, the main purpose of rounding for outcomes on teachers is to develop relationships with them. School leaders should open any rounding session by genuinely engaging in a conversation with the teacher. Be sure to address something that is meaningful or that is relevant to the teacher's present experiences. Then ask:

- What is working well today?
- Are there any individuals I should be recognizing?
- Do you have the tools and equipment you need to do your job?
- Is there anything we could do to improve?

Rounding allows school leaders to gain insight on what techniques are working for teachers, which teachers deserve to be recognized, and what tools and equipment teachers don't have but need in order to do their jobs in the best way possible.

An important side note: Rounding should not include what Studer Group calls we/they conversations. Do not engage in a discussion with a teacher who extends blame or points fingers at others in order to make herself look better. If this occurs, end the conversation. Let the teacher know why the conversation must end, and ask the teacher to focus on her own needs during the next rounding session. Tell her that by using the rounding time to "point the finger" or play blame games, she is wasting her time.

After each rounding session, record the information you receive from teachers in a log, make a note of those items that require action, and find a way to recognize those individuals whose achievements were highlighted by teachers during the discussions.

Many leaders learn during their rounding sessions that the items their employees need to do their jobs better are really very basic. Leaders often have no idea that those items were needed. When they hear about the need, they quickly solve the problem.

To illustrate this point, Quint Studer tells a story about red construction paper. The story shows how rounding could have prevented a negative situation.

Here is how the story goes: Several school districts serve as pilot sites for implementing the Studer Group strategies in their schools. An elementary teacher in one of the school districts talked to Studer about a situation at her school. Valentine's Day was fast approaching when the teachers went to the school supply closet and discovered the school was out of red construction paper. Angered and frustrated, the teachers complained about the leader not ordering red construction paper so close to Valentine's Day. They were in disbelief that a leader could be so insensitive.

Finally, one teacher asked the others if anyone had asked the school leader if she knew the school was out of red construction paper. After shaking their heads no, one of the teachers decided to make the request. Lo and behold, when the teacher asked the school leader, she said that she had no idea the school was out of red construction paper, and she placed the order immediately so that the new supply would arrive in time for Valentine's Day activities. Studer jokes that the Valentine's incident most likely occurred after the teachers experienced a blue and green Christmas!

Just think. If the school leader in the story had known about the benefits of rounding, the incident above and the negative feelings that came with it could have been avoided. She would have known long before their desperate need that she needed to order red construction paper. She could have been proactive about finding a solution. The energy the teachers spent on feeling angry and discontented could have been transferred to more positive behaviors.

Rounding is one of the most important actions school leaders can perform. However, for the practice to be successful, it must be scheduled in a consistent way. School leaders should place a high level of importance on rounding and should make sure they round on each of their teachers at least once a month. Some school leaders at large schools assign their assistant principal a group of teachers if they think they will not be able to get around to all of the teachers in a given month.

Based on our work with teacher learning teams, we've put together another way for school leaders to gain access to rounding information through teacher learning teams. However, we do not encourage leaders to replace their rounding plan with the one we provide. Rather, we propose that leaders use our method in addition to their own rounding methods.

Here's how it works: Each year we work with teacher learning teams in high need schools. A learning team consists of three to five teachers with one member serving as the coach. Depending on how the teams are formed, the coach can remain the same all year, or the teachers on a given team can take turns being the coach during the school year. The team member serving as coach rounds on the other team members. Rounding is always done in person rather than by email or other forms of written communication. The coach meets with the team of teachers and rounds on them at least once a month.

She completes a Rounding Log (Figure 4.1) for each teacher on the team. The coach compiles the information from the team and places the information on a Scouting Report (Figure 4.2) that is sent to the school leader each month. The school leader reviews the information, analyzes the responses to all the questions, notes the requests made by teachers so that she can provide feedback on each one, and recognizes those teachers or coaches whose great work was highlighted in the Scouting Report.

Figure 4.1. Rounding Log

Rounding Log	
Completed by Teacher Learning Team Coach for all Team Teachers	
Name of Teacher:	Date Rounding Completed:
Questions	Comments
Working well	
Individuals to recognize	
Tools and equipment needed	
Anything need to improve	

Adapted with permission from Studer Group, 2001 ©

Figure 4.2 Scouting Report

Scouting Report
Completed by Coach to Give to Principal
Date:
To:
From:
RE: Scouting Report
Things that are working well: Materials/Resources needed to do job: Things that could work better:

Adapted with permission from Studer Group, 2001 ©

Naturally, there are many ways to recognize your exemplary teachers. However, Studer recommends that leaders mail handwritten thank-you notes to employees. The notes should specifically identify the behavior that was recognized by others or by the leader. As you'll see below, Ms. Tucker used a thank-you note to reward and recognize one of her teachers, Ms. Wilson, for something her peer recognized on the Scouting Report.

Ms. Tucker, principal of Warrington Elementary School in Pensacola, Florida, received a Scouting Report from one of the coaches on the fifth grade team. On the Scouting Report the coach recognized that Ms. Wilson helped the fifth grade team run more efficient meetings. Ms. Tucker recognized the teacher by providing a thank-you note. In the thank-you note, Ms. Tucker wrote:

> Dear Ms. Wilson:
>
> I want to thank you for helping the fifth grade team have more efficient grade level meetings. Your great plan of having an agenda and response sheet really helps the team make the best use of their planning time. Carolyn Gambles also mentions your constant enthusiasm and daily positive outlook. Thank you for contributing to making our school better!
>
> Sincerely,
> Peggy Tucker

The Difference Between Classroom Walk-throughs and Rounding

Some leaders ask us why they need to round when they are already doing classroom walk-throughs. The reason is simple: The two practices are actually very different. When used effectively, classroom walk-throughs are a great way to guide teachers to reflect on their instructional strategies. Rounding, on the other hand, is an essential strategy for retaining teachers, and when it is hard-wired in an organization, it leads to great results.

When doing a walk-through, leaders or teams enter a teacher's classroom for three to five minutes and record what they see based on a specific set of indicators or behaviors. The observer and teacher then meet to discuss the instructional strategies recorded during that three- to five-minute interval.

As with most initiatives, some classroom walk-throughs work well and others do not. Some leaders do them well; others do not. Some see meaning in the walk-throughs; others do not. For some, walk-throughs have become so cumbersome that they have lost their purpose. Others more closely align to a process that has a proven track record, such as the method we recommend, the original classroom walk-through model developed by Carol Downey 40 years ago.

Nonetheless, the questions leaders ask when they round and the indicators observers use during classroom walk-throughs are very different. Figure 4.3 shows the rounding questions and Carol Downey's Classroom Walk-through questions side by side. We see value in Carol Downey's questions and use the content of the questions in Tactic 14.

Figure 4.3. Difference Between Rounding for Outcomes and Classroom Walk-through Questions

Quint Studer's Rounding for Outcomes Questions	Carol Downey's Classroom Walk-through Questions
• What is working well today? • Are there any individuals I should be recognizing? • Do you have the tools and equipment you need to do your job? • Is there anything we could do to improve?	• Are students instructionally oriented? • Are the lesson objectives aligned to standards and curriculum? Are the learning objectives apparent? • Do instructional strategies align to the objectives? What instructional decisions has the teacher made? • Do the walls of the classroom support meaningful learning? • Do you see anything that could be a safety hazard?

Another major difference between rounding and walk-throughs is that leaders do not enter teachers' classrooms while they are teaching. They choose a time that affords them an opportunity to engage in a conversation with the teacher to determine what's working well and what tools and equipment are needed.

Teachers enter their classrooms every day with one goal: to help students learn. Great school leaders help teachers achieve this goal. When leaders round they show teachers that they are committed to helping them become high performing teachers. Leaders and teachers build relationships with each other. They care about each others' well-being. Like students, teachers can't perform well when they do not know what is expected of them and have no opportunity to engage in discussions with their school leaders and peers. They may even decide to leave the school or, tragically, the profession.

Studer stresses that if leaders choose to embrace only one tactic from this entire book, it should be rounding on employees. Based on work the organization has done with healthcare organizations over the years, Studer Group research shows that rounding is one of the most important things leaders do to improve employee performance and satisfaction.

When the practice is hardwired in schools, it can have the same positive results.

1

Tactics 1-4:
When Teachers Know What to Expect, They Perform

- School leaders who don't try to reform their low performing teachers spend more time dealing with the problems associated with them than with supporting and coaching middle performing teachers and acknowledging high performers.

- School leaders should first hold conversations with high performing teachers, then middle performing teachers, and lastly low performers. Following this order shows teachers that high performance is valued and recognized.

- High performing teachers do not want to work with low performers. When low performance is not dealt with by the school leaders, the performance level of teachers as a whole will decline.

- Only about 8 percent of employees in an organization are low performers, and most of those low performers will improve or change negative behaviors to positive ones when addressed by the leader.

- Ignoring low performance does not make it go away. Leaders should provide clear expectations of performance and opportunities to change negative actions that lead to poor performance.

- High and middle performing teachers deserve for the majority of the leader's time to be spent with them rather than with low performers who refuse to change.

- School leaders use peer interviewing to hire the right teachers in the right places.

- Peer interviews include questions that focus on Tactics 5-14. Peer teachers ask the candidates to respond to performance- and behavior-based questions to determine if the candidates hold student learning and parent satisfaction as primary goals in their classrooms.

- School leaders hold 30- and 90-day meetings with new teacher hires to show that they are committed to keeping them at the school. At the end of 30 days, school leaders ask:
  - How do we compare to what we said we would be like?
  - Tell me what you like. What is going well?
  - I noticed you came to us from _____. Are there things you did there that might be helpful to us?
  - Is there anything here that you are uncomfortable with?

- At the 90-day meeting, the school leaders ask the 30-day questions plus two more:
  - Is there anyone you know who might be a valuable addition to our team?
  - As your supervisor, how can I be helpful?

- Rounding for outcomes on teachers shows them that school leaders care about their well-being and allows leaders to be proactive about solving problems. Leaders create a meaningful conversation with teachers and ask four questions:
  - What is working well today?
  - Are there any individuals I should be recognizing?
  - Do you have the tools and equipment you need to do your job?
  - Is there anything we could do better?

• School leaders should hardwire rounding and round with teachers at least once a month.

Principle 2:
What Teachers Permit in Their Classrooms, They Promote

Just as school leaders must connect the dots for teachers, teachers must connect the dots for students. It's important that students know what systems are in place, why the systems are important, and the consequences attached to not following them. But before teachers can connect the dots for their students, they need to understand where their students are falling short of the ideal—and they need to recognize their *own* role in allowing these behavior problems. To help leaders connect the dots for their employees, Studer Group® encourages them to ask, "What am I permitting, and thus promoting?" What leaders discover when they answer that question for themselves may surprise and disappoint them, but when they change their course of action based on their answer, they create opportunities to improve.

The good news is that teachers and students want the same things. In our work in schools, we hear from students that they want well-managed and well-organized classrooms. Students have more opportunities to learn when teachers help them connect the dots that set the stage for learning. Naturally, teachers, as leaders of their classrooms, expect students to follow rules and exhibit good behavior. However, if teachers permit certain student behaviors that do not align with their expectations, they send the message to students that those behaviors are acceptable. In other words, what they are permitting, they are promoting.

For example, when teachers have set forth a rule and a specific consequence for breaking that rule, they should consistently apply that consequence. Otherwise they are promoting students breaking the rule. If a teacher expects her students to hand in their papers in a certain way but then allows some students to do it differently, she is essentially saying, "The paper-handing-in rule is not really a rule, but a suggestion. Do it if you feel like it." Consistently applying rules and procedures lets students know what is and is not permitted in the classroom.

In order to develop better learning environments for their students, teachers must start permitting *only* those practices and behaviors that they want to promote with students and with their parents. Teacher interactions with students and parents prior to school and during the first week of school set the stage for an entire school year.

Consistently applying classroom management plans during the school year makes it possible for students to take control of their own behaviors. Chapters 5 and 6 focus on two essential tactics school leaders must use to help their teachers ensure they start the school year off right. The tactics will help teachers connect the dots for students and parents so that they all know what is expected from the first day of school to the end of the year. The two tactics center on maximizing parent-teacher interactions and applying classroom rules and procedures from day one.

CHAPTER 5

Tactic 5:
Coach Teachers on How to Maximize
Parent-Teacher Interactions

Why Tactic 5 Is Important

Zappos.com is an internet retail company that sells all brands of shoes. It has a 365-day return policy. In three years it ranked 79 out of the top 500 retail companies and grew financially by 948 percent. CEO of Zappos.com, Tony Hsieh, created a "service" rather than "shoe" company. He says that when hiring, Zappos chooses the person who is right for the company's culture, which doesn't necessarily mean he will be passionate about selling shoes. Rather, the company hires people who are passionate about providing customers with great service. Its staff does everything they can to instill loyalty in their customers so that they keep coming back to shop at Zappos.com.

Educators do not necessarily think about their students' parents as being customers of the services they are providing to their students each day. In fact, some educators resist identifying those they serve in education as customers. But similarities can be drawn—mainly, that if you develop a relationship with your students' parents, they will be more willing to work with you throughout the school year.

Though the type of service teachers provide to parents does not look the same as retail companies' service to customers, teachers and school leaders can learn from the success stories of certain companies, such as Zappos.com, because of their customer service commitments and achievements. Student learning and parent satisfaction results are key principles making up school accountability systems. We borrow from those business world customer service principles to create a tactic that makes our classrooms better and gives students better opportunities to learn.

Let's start by taking a look at a tactic that will help teachers garner improved parent satisfaction results.

Teacher-parent communication is usually infrequent and usually occurs when the teacher is having difficulty with a youngster. The situation usually plays out like this. A teacher calls a parent and informs her that her child is misbehaving in class. The teacher then expects the parent to handle the situation so that the negative behavior changes. Unfortunately, that rarely happens.

Because the teacher spends every day with the child's negative behavior, she feels very frustrated and expects the child's parents to feel the same level of frustration. However, it can be difficult for the parent to feel the teacher's pain, and when that doesn't happen, the teacher usually becomes even more frustrated, now at the student *and* the parent.

Consequently, the parent-teacher relationship sours, and the parent then starts to feel that it is less important to work with the teacher on solving the problem, especially when she gets call after call after call from the teacher. Parents look at the caller ID, cringe at the thought of again interacting with the frustrated teacher, and/or choose not to answer for fear of more bad news.

Teachers must learn how to have welcoming and genuine interaction with the parents of their students. When they do so, they are helping to make their classroom a performance-driven learning environment rather than a compliance-driven learning environment. We use these two terms to provide examples (performance-driven classrooms) and non-examples (compliance-driven classrooms) of Tactics 5 to 14 when being applied by teachers. These illustrations help school leaders know when they need to coach teachers on how to improve and when they should recognize and reward great teaching. When leaders and teachers are knowledgeable about the tactics that produce results, both can work together to make classrooms great places for students to learn.

Teachers should make parents feel that they have a place in their child's education. In performance-driven classrooms, parents feel that the teacher cares to know them, understands their needs regarding their child, and believes they and their child are important. Of course, this kind of parent-teacher relationship does not automatically occur. Teachers need to do particular things at the beginning of each year to build a genuine relationship with parents. In fact, the process should begin before students enter the classroom on the first day of school. It begins with two teacher actions: 1) Contacting parents prior to the beginning of the school year, and 2) Contacting parents during the year with compliments about their child.

As with students, parents come from diverse backgrounds and are not always easy to connect with. Also, some students might have adults other than parents who serve as their caregivers. Others may have parents who are difficult to get in touch with. No matter the situation, each parent or caregiver is important and deserves an opportunity to be part of a performance-driven classroom. School leaders shouldn't accept any excuses from teachers who don't do their due diligence by making serious attempts to connect with parents, knowing what parents value, and explaining the classroom procedures and teacher expectations.

Sharing good news is important if teachers want parents to help them handle any negative student behaviors. Years of research by the Gallup Organization shows that on average it takes three compliments to one criticism to get a positive result from customers. It takes three compliments to one criticism to invoke a positive behavior, two compliments to one criticism to invoke a neutral behavior, and one compliment to one criticism to invoke a negative behavior.

When teachers practice the "three compliments to one criticism" principle with parents so that they hear good things about their children, parents are much more willing to do something about the negative behavior if and when it occurs.

Teachers need to connect, listen, and respond to parents. Parents may not be "customers," but they certainly should be partners. When teachers develop partnerships with parents, they welcome the parents to the school year, listen carefully to understand their situations and needs, and remain mindful that parents need to hear good stories about their children. Think what parents can do to help teachers work with students to get the same annual growth that Zappos achieved—an average 300 percent annual growth rate!

How to Apply Tactic 5

Before school begins, parents are a little anxious. Generally, parents do not get to select their child's teacher. They must simply hope that their child is assigned a great teacher.

Tactic 5, coaching teachers on how to maximize parent-teacher interactions, is meant to help teachers develop partnerships with their students' parents. Teachers do this by calling parents and/or by requesting that parents complete parent preference cards.

To get the year off to a good start, teachers need to make an effort to reach every parent or caregiver prior to the first day students enter the classroom. Keep in mind that some parents may be easy to reach by phone while others may need teachers to visit them in person. Either way, connecting with parents prior to the school year can reduce their anxiety and let them know that the teacher cares about them and believes that their input is important.

Make Parent Phone Calls

Some teachers may be at a loss as to exactly how these parent interactions should go. That's why we once again look to Studer Group's work with healthcare organizations to find an answer. Using a process it developed, Studer Group has helped its clients find great success with increasing patient satisfaction using a process that makes patients feel more comfortable. In fact, at Advocate Good Samaritan Hospital, in a little over a year, outpatient satisfaction shifted from about 30 percent to 96 percent when the staff started using AIDET.

Studer Group suggests using five fundamentals of service called AIDET. The letters stand for Acknowledge, Introduce, Duration, Explanation, and Thank you. Teachers can use the AIDET approach when contacting parents before the first day of school and during the school year.

When using the AIDET approach, teachers should first acknowledge the parent by name. The teacher then introduces herself, her skill set, and educational training, so the parent can have confidence in the teacher and the experience her child will have during the year. The teacher describes what is going to happen in the first week and first 30 days of school and then goes into more detail on why this is important. The teacher then ends the conversation and thanks the parent.

Sample AIDET for Teacher and Parent Conversation

Acknowledge	Hello, Ms. Green. I am Ms. Smith, and I am going to be Deron's teacher this year. I want this year to be the best school year that he has ever had.
Introduce	Ms. Green, I want you to know that I am a certified teacher and enjoy working at our neighborhood school. I have been a successful teacher here for five years.
Duration	Ms. Green, together, we can help Deron learn this year. This week he will bring home our classroom procedures that we will all follow to ensure that every student can learn.
Explanation	At the end of the first 30 days of school, I am going to send a parent survey to you by giving it to Deron. This will give you a chance to provide feedback to me about how you think Deron is doing.
Thank you	Thank you for being part of our school. I look forward to working with you and Deron this year. If you have any questions, you can contact me at this number, _____. Is this the best way to contact you? Have a good day, Ms. Green.

Adapted with permission from © Studer Group, LLC

When applying AIDET with a parent, the teacher indicates that she will follow up with the parent at the end of 30 days by sending home a brief survey to gather the parent's input about her child's experiences in class. In addition to the AIDET conversation, during the school year teachers should harvest student wins with parents by using the three compliments to one criticism principle. Teachers should call about three to five parents a week to tell them something good that happened in class with their children.

Note that this practice also allows teachers to keep the lines of communication open with parents. Using the AIDET approach to make an initial phone call and then following up with positive phone calls encourages parents to become partners with teachers.

Parents want to believe teachers care about them and their children. Tactic 5 immediately shows parents that teachers care about making them partners in their children's learning. When teachers connect with parents, listen to their feedback, and harvest wins with their children, teachers will receive more positive than negative feedback from parents.

We find that teachers who use this approach get a huge boost in building parent relationships because parents are not accustomed to teachers making that initial contact. Parents feel less anxious and more excited about the possibilities for their children as they begin the school year. After receiving that initial phone call, parents feel lucky that their child is in a great teacher's classroom. When teachers continue to make positive phone calls, a parent's impression that her child has a great teacher is reinforced.

Prior to school beginning, teachers create a relationship with parents. When students arrive on the first day of school, students will learn, practice, and apply classroom rules and classroom procedures (Tactic 6). Because the parent-teacher relationships have already been formed, parents will be ready and willing to help teachers reinforce the rules and procedures of the classroom.

Parent Preference Cards

As the CEO of a healthcare organization, Studer introduced preference cards to his staff. Physicians complete preference cards for the nursing staff to review. The nurses are then able to meet the needs of physicians, and, in turn, patients receive the best possible care. In addition to following physician preferences, nurses place patient preferences on a white board in the patients' rooms.

Applying this approach to classrooms allows teachers to connect with parents in another meaningful way. Chris Renouf, the principal of Toledo Blade Elementary School in Sarasota, Florida, has created a model for hardwiring excellence in his school. The teachers at Toledo Blade ask parents to complete a parent preference card that asks them (among other things) what they want the teacher to know about their children and how they prefer to be reached when teachers need to communicate with them. This enables teachers to let parents know that they value and respect them, that their children are in good hands, and that they want to connect with them efficiently.

Tactic 5 encourages teachers to connect with parents as soon as possible in order to get the school year off to a good start. It also encourages teachers to continue connecting with parents during the school year to harvest student wins. When teachers follow Tactic 5, parents become partners with teachers in their children's learning.

School leaders must coach teachers on how to apply the AIDET approach to call parents prior to the beginning of school, make about three to five weekly phone calls to different parents, and request that parents complete parent preference cards. These actions help build healthy parent-teacher relationships and provide students with better opportunities to achieve student learning results.

Parent Preference Card **Bakerfield High School**
Parent Name: Mary Ann Leevon
What is the best way to communicate with you during the school year? Please use my cell phone number because I travel a lot for my job, (123) 456-7890. Also, you should know that Perry stays with my parents when I travel. Their number is (123) 456-7891.
I'd like for us to work together during the school year on recognizing those things Perry does well. What are his strengths? Perry loves working on the computer and is very creative with designing technology tools. He also is very kind to others and is sensitive when others hurt his feelings, although he does not like to show or admit this aspect of his personality.
What should I know about Perry that could help him learn in the best way possible? Perry is very shy and does not always demonstrate his best work. I am hopeful that his confidence will increase if he experiences success this year.

Adapted with permission from © Studer Group, LLC

Tactic 6:
Coach and Support Teachers as They Apply Classroom Rules and Procedures

Why Tactic 6 Is Important

Harry Wong has spent much of his life on the road talking to large groups of teachers. His message? That the first days of school make or break a teacher for the entire school year. Harry and Rosemary Wong elaborate on that point in their book, *The First Days of School*, the first two versions of which have sold over 2 million copies. The third edition continues to sell at rocket speed.

If you haven't read *The First Days of School*, please do so. The strategies the authors recommend have worked for thousands of teachers. Implementing their strategies can mean the difference between having a good year with your students or a year in which you are constantly looking for a way to manage their behavior.

Tactic 6 is inspired by chapters 18, 19, and 20 of *The First Days of School*. These chapters cover classroom rules, consequences, and procedures aimed at creating effective learning environments. More details and examples for elementary, middle, and high school teachers can be found in that book. Again, it is definitely worth a read, though we will hit some of the high spots here.

Classroom rules and procedures provide students with guidelines on how they are expected to behave in class. Wong continuously stresses that teachers need to develop a classroom management plan. The plan should consist of both classroom rules and procedures.

School leaders need to make sure teachers establish and communicate classroom rules, the consequences for breaking the rules, and the rewards for following the rules on the very first day of school. Procedures concern how various tasks and exercises will be performed in a classroom. School leaders should additionally reinforce that teachers teach, rehearse, practice, and assess classroom procedures with their students.

Here are examples of both a classroom rule with its consequences and a procedure. Notice the difference between the two.

Rule: Turn in non-graded assignments on time.

Consequences:
- For the *first* assignment not turned in or turned in late, students get a verbal warning.
- For the *second* assignment not turned in or turned in late, students complete a pink slip identifying their negative behavior and make a commitment statement, saying they will follow the rule for the remainder of the grading period.
- For the *third* assignment not turned in or turned in late, students will be assigned to detention where they are expected to complete the missing work.

Procedure: As you enter the classroom, turn in homework in the blue box on the front table.

There are no negative consequences associated with classroom procedures. Rather, teachers teach, rehearse, practice, and assess procedures with their students at the beginning of the year, and if during the year students demonstrate they cannot apply appropriate classroom procedures, teachers re-establish them.

Wong has discovered from his own classroom and the classrooms of the many teachers he has observed that students learn the best when they develop a clear understanding of classroom procedures in the very first week of the school year. To get the school year off to a good start, school leaders must coach and support teachers as they apply classroom rules and procedures starting on the first day of school.

How to Apply Tactic 6

The First Days of School opens with an overview of what Douglas Brooks discovered through his research in the mid '80s. Brooks observed a group of teachers and found that when teachers started their first day of school with a fun activity, they spent the rest of the year trying to manage their students' poor behavior. The most effective teachers started the day by reviewing how the classroom was going to be organized and structured. They also made sure their students understood how to be productive members of the class.

Like Studer, the Wongs believe in hardwiring these types of behaviors. In bold letters in their book they highlight the following phrase, "The most important thing to establish the first week of school is consistency."

Classroom Rules and Consequences

Before school begins, teachers create classroom rules, which spell out their expectations of appropriate classroom behavior for a given year's students. The rules should represent the desired behaviors that are the most important to the teacher. Teachers should make it clear that students **choose** to follow or break rules. If and when students break a rule, specific hierarchical consequences occur for them. The rules and their consequences need to be clearly communicated verbally, posted in the classroom, and taught to students.

The Wongs suggest that each classroom should have no more than five rules and provide a thorough explanation of why in their book. Basically, students can easily remember five rules, and teachers want students to remember them every day. Also, students who see value in no more than five rules are apt to follow the number of rules that seems reasonable to them.

Rules can be general or specific and should be appropriate to the grade level taught. Note that general rules provide teachers with more flexibility, but they must be carefully taught to students. While specific rules define very specific behaviors, with only five, they do not allow for the same flexibility.

It is also important to note that students must also follow district- and school-wide sets of rules. Teachers should also cover these rules with students and make sure they understand the consequences of breaking them.

Let's look at an example: Ms. Lee, a high school history teacher, has three general rules for her students. They are: Be productive, be respectful to others, and be on time to class. Ms. Lee highly values these three rules. She believes that when students choose to break one of the rules, they should receive a consequence for their selected behavior.

To ensure her students understand the classroom rules, she spends the first week of school teaching what it means to be productive and respectful. She also explains what it means to be on time to class. She uses a lot of non-examples for the last rule. She tells students that being on time to class means "sitting in your seat" doing the "bell work" posted on the board. It does not mean a toe in the door, sliding into the room at high speed, or running to your desk.

Ms. Lee also teaches and posts the consequences for breaking her rules. Harry Wong teaches that the cardinal principle when issuing consequences is to keep instruction moving. When you see a rule being broken, give out the penalty immediately without stopping instruction. Ms. Lee created index cards that have the rules and their consequences listed in sequential order. Each time a student breaks a rule, she puts an index card on the student's desk and he must check the rule that was broken and its corresponding consequence.

If it is a student's first offense, Ms. Lee issues a verbal warning at the end of class. For the second offense, the student receives a slip on which the student must describe how his behavior needs to change. The student is then expected to meet with Ms. Lee after school to discuss the behavior change. On the third offense, the student completes the slip again, takes it home to his parents, and Ms. Lee makes a parent phone call. On the fourth offense, the student receives 30 minutes after-school detention. On the fifth offense, the student is sent to the dean's office. And because the student is completing an index card each time a rule is broken, he knows exactly where he stands at all times.

Ms. Lee keeps a file that includes each student's name. As rules are broken, she places the index cards behind the offending student's name. Every day she can see the number of cards each student has in the file box. Ms. Lee's system is only one of many possible examples for how teachers can establish rules and consequences for breaking them.

Classroom Procedures

Developing and applying classroom rules are important teacher actions. But Harry Wong says the number one problem in classrooms is not discipline.

Rather, teachers face the most problems when their classrooms lack procedures and routines. He stresses that the chapter on classroom procedures is the most important one in his book, and Harry Wong spends most of his time during presentations talking about classroom procedures.

Behavior problems are usually caused by teachers who lack classroom procedures. Students are open and accepting of clearly understood classroom procedures because the procedures help them succeed. Students do not like classrooms that are chaotic or classrooms where teachers must constantly yell at and discipline students in order to get them on task.

Harry Wong defines a procedure as something a teacher wants done. A procedure will eventually become a classroom routine. It is a task or exercise students automatically do without being prompted or supervised by the teacher. Procedures must be explained and demonstrated, rehearsed by students, and reinforced by the teacher through re-teaching and practicing until they become routine. Teachers should teach, rehearse, and reinforce classroom procedures with students before they begin teaching content during that first week of school.

Most teachers have procedures for the following areas: how the class should be working when the bell rings, how the students are to be dismissed from class, how to get students' attention, how students are to ask the teacher a question, how students are to request permission to exit the room, how students are to turn in work (classwork and homework), how student absences are handled, and how students are to label their papers.

Procedures do not have consequences. If a student fails to follow the procedure, the teacher asks the student to explain the procedure that was not followed. If a number of students fail to follow the procedure, the teacher re-teaches and practices the procedure with the class until they are clear about how to follow the procedure.

Harry Wong's daughter-in-law, Cindy Wong, used a five-step procedure to quiet her sixth grade classroom, which has been adopted by many other teachers. She started by raising one hand with one finger showing, which indicates the students should have their eyes on the speaker. Two fingers mean be quiet. Three fingers mean be still. Four fingers mean stop what you're doing. Five fingers mean listen. She practiced using the finger system until the students learned the five steps. After the students had been taught and rehearsed the procedure, Ms. Wong would say, "Give me five." The middle school youngsters would go through each of the five steps in their minds. It took Ms. Wong no more than five seconds to gain their attention by simply stating, "Give me five."

Teachers Starting the School Year off Right

Each teacher creates his own rules and classroom procedures and introduces them to his students on the very first day of school. Teachers create three to five rules and the sequential consequences for breaking the rules. They clearly communicate the expectations for following the rules and the consequences for students who do not. Teachers also create, teach, rehearse, and reinforce classroom procedures, which have no consequences attached. The teacher understands that classroom procedures create a learning environment that helps students achieve academic success.

As previously mentioned, each year we work with teams of teachers who teach in high need schools. We help them plan and implement their plans for the first 30 days of school. As part of our program, we ask that our teachers produce evidence at the end of the first week of school that all students in their classrooms are able to practice the classroom procedures.

After they've taught the rules and procedures and students have practiced them, the teachers administer an assessment that includes both a paper-and-pencil test and a performance assessment. Teachers created a paper-and-pencil test on the classroom rules and procedures that students take during the first week with the expectation that all students score 100 percent. They also assess their students by watching their behaviors and documenting their performance.

Almost all of the teachers we worked with said that adding the assessment of classroom rules and procedures was one of the most valuable things learned. They told us they saw value in having a tool that helped them reassess students when they were not following rules or practicing the classroom procedures.

When teachers practice Tactic 6, students are ready to learn during the first week of school. Students feel comfortable and safe, and, therefore, eager to begin the year. When new students arrive in teachers' classrooms, the teachers teach, practice, rehearse, and assess classroom rules and procedures. If at any time the teacher feels students are forgetting rules and procedures, he can choose to teach, practice, rehearse, and assess them again. When teachers know that they can re-teach and re-assess rules and procedures, they are able to build confidence in their abilities to create well-managed classrooms.

When students follow classroom rules and procedures, Harry Wong says that teachers need to recognize and reward them. We agree. In our work with teachers, we have seen positive results when teachers take time to harvest the wins of students by recognizing and rewarding success. We believe in harvesting the wins to get student results and have included this action as an essential tactic discussed later in the book.

Tactics 5-6:
What Teachers Permit in Their Classrooms, They Promote

To achieve improved student learning and parent satisfaction results, school leaders must coach teachers to:

• Use the AIDET approach to call parents before the school year to welcome their children to the class and invite the parents to be partners in the student learning process. The teacher applies the actions below:

> A—Acknowledge. Acknowledges the parent.
> I—Introduce. Introduces herself, her skill set, and educational training.
> D—Duration. Describes what is going to happen during the first 30 days of school.
> E—Explanation. Explains why the first 30 days are important.
> T—Thank you. Thanks the parents for the opportunity to teach their children.

• Ask parents to complete parent preference cards that provide teachers with information about their children's learning preferences and also asks how parents prefer to be contacted.

- Give, on average, three compliments for every one criticism in order to get positive results.

- Make about three to five positive phone calls to recognize and reward student success each week throughout the year.

- Create, communicate, teach, and assess classroom rules and their consequences for students.

- Teach, rehearse, practice, and assess classroom procedures. Teachers do not attach negative consequences for students not following procedures. Rather, they re-teach, re-assess, and ask students to repeat the correct procedure.

Principle 3:
What Teachers Measure, Students Value

We believe that young people and adults want to live lives of purpose, do worthwhile work, and in some way make a difference in the world. Teachers want to make a difference in the lives of their students. Indeed, the desire to perform meaningful work is a human need that transcends age and industry.

A graphic created by Studer—an organizational flywheel that serves as the centerpiece of his work with clients in all fields—shows how this need drives performance. The hub of his flywheel is "purpose, worthwhile work, and making a difference." He teaches that when an organization helps employees reconnect to their passion to do worthwhile work, they are inspired to put in place tactics that turn the flywheel faster and faster until it gains momentum that is unstoppable.

These three values—purpose, worthwhile work, and making a difference—drive most people to desire to become better at what they do.

To become better, people need to know where they are going and what is expected of them. Likewise, for students to learn, they need to know what they should be focusing on and what they should do in order to reach a desired goal. Therefore, teachers need to be very strategic about what they measure and how they coach students to achieve the desired goals defined by the measures.

Performance-driven classrooms hold these same three values—purpose, worthwhile work, and making difference—which serve as the glue that holds the framework of the tactics together. Teachers enter classrooms with the goal of helping their students find their sense of purpose and do worthwhile work. Consequently, students take more ownership of their learning.

In performance-driven classrooms, teachers no longer need to read about and attempt various creative ways for motivating students. The renewed passion the students have for learning and the sense of purpose they gain from their classroom experience breed self-motivation.

In his work with teachers, Rick Stiggins has found that when teachers apply assessments as students are learning, their students become more engaged and take control of their own learning. Harry Wong also provides numerous examples of students, whose ability to learn improves when their teachers connect the dots for them and create a classroom where they clearly understand classroom procedures and learning expectations. And from the evidence that Studer reveals in his work with healthcare organizations, we can safely surmise that teachers can reconnect to students' eagerness to learn when they create a classroom culture built around the core principles of "purpose, worthwhile work, and making a difference."

For their part, school leaders need to understand that for this to happen teachers have to be coached and receive the support they'll need in order to put old habits aside and build excellence in their classrooms. The first step for teachers is knowing how to apply the tactics. They then have to commit to, and continuously work on, the tactics in their classrooms to keep the momentum going until finally the culture of the classroom changes.

There is a defining difference between teachers in performance-driven classrooms and those in compliance-driven classrooms. Teachers in performance-driven classrooms expect excellence, while teachers in compliance-driven classrooms expect perfection. By holding their students to a standard of perfection, teachers in compliance-driven classrooms set them up for failure. Teachers should build a culture of excellence instead—a culture that accepts mistakes and uses them as learning experiences.

Studer says that most employees serve their organization in one of two capacities: "renter" or "owner." Renters determine their responsibilities based on the specifics of their job description. Anything falling outside of those responsibilities is someone else's problem. Owners, on the other hand, know that what they do affects the organization and their place in it. They do whatever they can to keep improving the organization.

In the education world, performance-driven classrooms create places where students are owners of their learning rather than renters. Students who are renters do their assignments only because they will receive a reward or punishment in the form of a grade. Owners, however, want to learn because they want to improve and see the value in creating a classroom environment in which everyone is working from the same frame of reference. Owner students learn without being reminded to do so, while renters have to be told over and over again to do the tasks so that they do not receive a failing grade.

Years ago, Robbie Langford sat in the front row of a geometry class at Woodham High School. Robbie was in no way a star student. He often struggled, as many students do. Initially, he had a poor attitude about math, especially geometry. Each day, his teacher spoke with Robbie and his classmates about making progress one step at a time and by reaching one defined learning target each day. Everyone learned together, practiced together, made mistakes together, and helped each other correct and understand their mistakes. Many of the students never saw the relevance of geometry, but they did see the relevance of achieving the daily learning target.

During the year, Robbie got better and better and more confident about his ability to do math. He left that year loving rather than hating math. Years later, Robbie, a former student of Janet's, was walking down the hall at the university where we now teach. Robbie, it turns out, was studying to be a math teacher.

In our years of teaching, we have learned from the numerous stories just like this one to never underestimate the difference teachers can make in their students' lives. As with many of our students, we find that when teachers expect excellence from them and coach them to learn, the students own their learning. Our students are eager to learn and so are we.

Students long for teachers to spark a fire in them. When that occurs, teachers make a difference in their lives. Just like nurses and doctors, teachers hold the lives of their students in their hands. They determine if a child moves up to the 96th percentile or down to the 3rd percentile. The three tactics associated with Principle 3, and for that matter the tactics connected to each of our principles, provide some rather common-sense, essential actions that reinforce student learning.

In his most recent work, Rick Stiggins encourages teachers and leaders to see the value of allowing students to be part of the assessment process. That is, when including students in the assessment process, they become owners rather than renters of their learning. His research with his colleagues over the past three decades provides evidence that schools need to re-think the way learning is approached in their classrooms.

As discussed in the previous chapter, students want teachers to create rules and procedures to organize and structure the learning environment. Students have more opportunity for seeing "purpose" in learning when they are in classrooms that promote encouragement in place of obedience. Likewise, students gain motivation to learn when teachers coach students to achieve before they judge and grade them.

We need to understand that the three tactics associated with Principle 3 directly influence student learning results. Therefore, when we do not effectively apply Tactics 7, 8, and 9, some students have little room for achieving success in the classroom.

Tactic 7:
Help Teachers Create and Reach Measurable Learning Targets

Why Tactic 7 Is Important

When a young child learns to swim, the swimming teacher does not throw the child in the water and say "sink or swim." The teacher shows the child what the target looks like by swimming a few strokes, teaches the child the strategies, and works with the child one step at a time until she is able to swim a particular distance in a particular way. The teacher then increases the skill level of the target and helps the child build excellence in her approach and technique.

When the child makes a mistake, the teacher does not assign her a failing grade, yell at her, or punish her. Rather, the teacher carefully analyzes what she is doing incorrectly, tells her why it is incorrect, and shows the child how to correct it. The child leaves every day of swimming lessons eager to return because she wants to become a better and better swimmer. Together they work and work and work until the child is able to swim with good technique across the pool.

The moral of the story is that when teachers help students connect the dots between their work and the learning targets they are trying to achieve, students become more passionate about learning.

Young children enter their classroom on their very first day of school with the same eagerness to learn. Once they leave kindergarten, their learning experiences gradually begin to change. When students enter grades where accountability occurs, usually around second and third grades, teachers change the way they approach student learning. Starting with those grades, the stakes become high for teachers because state and district accountability systems mandate that students score at a particular level on standardized tests. In turn, teachers tend to create a high stakes learning environment for students. As a result, their hunger for learning gradually dissipates.

Students often finish a school year feeling defeated, understanding that the next school year will bring another series of seemingly irrelevant daily assignments. They lose their eagerness and natural desire for learning. They are no longer as proud of their accomplishments. And after 12 years many have entirely lost that eagerness to learn. Somewhere along the way, their teachers failed to connect the dots for them.

So how do teachers learn to connect the dots for their students? We use Stiggins's term, "learning target," as a way to build a visual for teachers as they work with students. Other familiar terms include *behavioral objectives, learning goals,* and *performance objectives.*

Learning targets include measurable capability actions students will be expected to perform. Measures define performance benchmarks of achievement. The learning target is much more meaningful when a measure is assigned to it. The learning targets guide the type of instruction that is needed to hit the target. The measure determines how well the student is doing.

Teachers need to create clear learning targets that are written in measurable terms, and they should attach measures to those targets. They also need to attach final measures to learning targets that are going to be assessed once students have had every opportunity to learn and practice the targets. Tactic 7 shows ways to create measurable learning targets.

If there are no measurements in place, teachers fail to know if students hit their learning targets. Teachers can use measurements to hold students accountable. They also let students know how close they are to hitting their learning targets. Teachers should not measure only because of mandates. Teachers should measure to help their students see where they are with regard to their learning goals. The better a teacher aligns the measure to a desired target, the faster students achieve results.

"Sticky Ball": A Lesson in Learning Targets and Measures

Think of the learning target being the bull's-eye of a dart board made up of five concentric circles. Students stand at a distance from the dart board and throw a sticky ball at the target. Let's say the bull's-eye represents the number "5," the highest achievement level. One circle out from the bull's-eye represents a "4," two circles out a "3," and so on. Naturally, the bull's-eye is the most difficult to hit because it is the smallest space on the diagram. The more students practice throwing the sticky ball at the target, the closer they get to hitting the bull's-eye until finally they hit it and continue to do so more consistently. Some students need more instruction, practice, and coaching than others. But everyone has an opportunity to hit the target.

When instruction begins, the teacher communicates the learning target to his students: "Demonstrate throwing the sticky ball with accuracy by hitting the bull's-eye 80 percent of the time." He then tells the group they are going to be expected to throw 25 sticky balls and hit the bull's-eye 80 percent of the time to get an "A" letter grade. The instructor first gives them some pointers on how to throw the sticky ball to gain accuracy. He then demonstrates how to throw a sticky ball. He asks them to practice so that he can coach them on how to throw the sticky ball. They are given a first assignment: Throw five sticky balls and hit the bull's-eye twice. When that is achieved, throw five balls and hit the bull's-eye three times. When that is achieved, in order to achieve an 80 percent accuracy rate, throw five sticky balls and hit the bull's-eye four times. For those struggling at the beginning, the instructor goes back and re-teaches the technique, demonstrates the behavior, and provides some encouragement. As the group continues to practice, the instructor carefully watches them. He determines who is struggling and coaches them on how to improve. For those doing well, the coach recognizes success and encourages their good performance. On the final assessment, the group is assessed at 80 percent accuracy for 25 throws. At a certain point, the instructor evaluates their performance. Those who hit the target 80 percent of the time in 25 throws receive an "A" letter grade. Others receive a grade based on a scale used for assigning grades. If the coach believes that too many students scored low on the test, the coach re-teaches the skill.

The final measure is for individuals to throw 25 sticky balls with an 80 percent accuracy rate. However, it should be noted that along the way small measures were provided to the group to help them know how they were doing and to motivate them to keep trying to get closer and closer to achieving the final goal. In addition to helping the students, the measures also provided the teacher with performance information so that he could determine if his teaching methods were working or if he needed to teach using a different strategy.

In performance-driven classrooms, measurements serve as a way to excite students when they see they are achieving. Frequent measures reinforce positive behaviors as long as those measures do not have punitive actions attached to them. Students can use the measures to know when and how to improve. Students who see that the measures are tied to their efforts to reach the learning target will strive harder to achieve as long as they are not punished when they are practicing.

Conversely, teachers in compliance-driven classrooms use measurements to keep students in line. Students are penalized by measures when they are trying to learn so they usually end up feeling defeated. Students who are motivated by grades simply do enough to meet the requirements dictated by the teacher. And students not motivated by grades will check out before trying to learn.

When engaging with workers, Studer recommends that measures be used to motivate employees and reinforce positive behaviors. School leaders must help teachers apply this concept in the classroom by encouraging them to consistently reinforce positive steps in student learning rather than punishing students for mistakes made during learning.

How to Apply Tactic 7

Benjamin Bloom, a well-known figure in the education world, identified six levels within the cognitive domain of learning. The levels start with "knowledge," and get increasingly complex, until the highest order of thinking, "evaluation," is reached. He also created capability verbs, which correspond with each level and which represent measurable behaviors students do in classrooms. Figure 7.1 provides the six levels and their measurable capability verbs.

Figure 7.1. Bloom's Taxonomy and Sample Measurable Verbs

Mental Levels	Sample Measurable Capability Verbs
Knowledge	arrange, define, duplicate, label, list, memorize, name, order, recognize, relate, recall, repeat, reproduce, state, sort
Comprehension	classify, describe, discuss, explain, express, identify, indicate, locate, recognize, report, restate, review, select, translate
Application	apply, choose, demonstrate, dramatize, employ, illustrate, interpret, operate, practice, schedule, sketch, solve
Analysis	analyze, appraise, calculate, categorize, compare, contrast, criticize, differentiate, discriminate, distinguish, examine, experiment, question, test
Synthesis	arrange, assemble, collect, compose, construct, create, design, develop, formulate, manage, organize, plan, prepare, propose
Evaluation	appraise, argue, assess, attach, choose, defend, estimate, judge, predict, rate, select, support, value, evaluate

Learning targets must contain a capability verb and an action. The verb indicates the skill level needed for a given task. It can also be observed. For example, you can determine when a student "states," "identifies," and "sorts" things. Note that sometimes the verbs "know" and "understand" are included in a taxonomy chart. We do not recommend that teachers use these two verbs because you cannot visually see what "know" and "understand" look like. But you can easily put measures on verbs that represent a very clear action. Here are several examples of learning targets:

- ***Arrange*** (capability verb) the given words in alphabetical order (action).
- ***Argue*** (capability verb) for or against two oppositional points (action).
- ***Select*** (capability verb) the correct solved linear equation (action).

Learning targets must also have measures attached to them. The measures help students determine if and when they have hit the learning target at the **acceptable** level defined by their teacher. The measures help the teacher understand what she needs to teach more or less of and which assessments will help her align the instruction to specific learning targets.

For example, when assessing the learning target, "argue for or against two oppositional points," teachers will need to create well-defined criteria for what it means to "argue" well and attach measures to the criteria to communicate to students what is expected of them. A teacher might create a 5-point scale to let students know how well they are doing at forming an acceptable argument. Remember, each of the levels needs a narrative description to clarify what it means.

Let's take a look at what occurs when teachers assess the writing skill "organization." Let's say that in one week a teacher wants students to demonstrate they can write a well-organized paragraph scoring at least a 4.0 level of accuracy on a 5-point scale. First, students need to know what is meant by a 4.0 accuracy level. The teacher provides the information in Figure 7.2 and then uses that information to guide the instruction and practice during the week.

Teachers need to clearly explain what is meant by the descriptors they use and need to clearly define the 1 to 5 scale and corresponding descriptions they use. In Figure 7.2, the scale starts with the highest level, "Hit above the target," and goes to the lowest level, "Begin again." The students use the measurable descriptors to determine what they need to do to write a well-organized paragraph. And the teacher uses the measurable descriptors to teach and demonstrate what a well-organized paragraph looks like. She uses the principles to coach students as they practice using the measures to get an overall 4.0 accuracy level.

Once they have practiced, the teacher gives the students two to three prompts and asks them to demonstrate writing a well-organized paragraph that she will assess and use to assign a grade. In this case, the teacher wants the student to get at least a 4.0 on all assessed areas. Students receive the highest grade when they achieve all 4s or above.

Figure 7.2. Scale of Measures for Writing a Well-Organized Paragraph

Descriptors	5 – Hit above the target	4 – Hit the target	3 – Re-do with minor revisions	2 – Re-do with major revisions	1 – Begin again
The paragraph has an introduction that gives the reader an indication of what the paragraph is going to be about.					
The conclusion leaves the reader with a sense of closure about the thoughts in the paragraph.					
Sequencing of thoughts is logical and effectively helps the reader know what the writer is describing.					
Transitions clearly connect one thought to another.					

© Janet K. Pilcher

Teachers create measures that are meaningful to them and that guide student learning. An alternate measure for the same activity could be that students will demonstrate that they can write a well-organized paragraph receiving 100 percent of their scores at either level 4 or 5. Teachers create measures that challenge students, but which are also realistic and achievable.

The teacher is in a position to make the best judgment about the learning target. She must determine what students can realistically achieve within a given time. To do this, teachers need to clearly express learning targets and measures, communicate to students what it means for them to achieve at the highest measure, and instruct, demonstrate, and help students practice hitting the learning targets at the stated measurable level. When this occurs, the school leader has confidence that students are learning in performance-based classrooms where they clearly understand what is expected of them.

CHAPTER

Tactic 8:
Help Teachers Create and Follow 30-Day Plans

Why Tactic 8 Is Important

States have created so many standards and benchmarks that teachers find it extremely difficult to "cover" them, much less determine how well students achieve them. States tend to have too many standards, which are not written in measurable terms. Put another way, the standards do not begin with a measurable verb such as those listed in Bloom's Taxonomy Chart, and they do not focus on one particular outcome.

We recommend that teachers carefully review and interpret the standards in their respective content areas to determine the knowledge and skills students need to demonstrate them. By doing so they can create a common list of skills that cut across standards in the content areas and most likely across subjects. When teachers complete this exercise, they usually come up with 10 to 15 common skills in a particular content area that they can work on throughout the year. This strategy enables students to practice those 10 to 15 skills many times before taking an end-of-year standardized achievement test.

Rather than completing the strategy above, however, teachers often feel pressured to "cover" material rather than report how well students learn. Harry Wong says that teachers who "cover" material rather than check for student understanding create an environment where students are much more likely to be off task and not learning.

To appropriately align instruction to standards, we encourage teachers to think about the state standards as guidelines for developing learning targets and measures. To help teachers do this, we created Lesson Architect™, a free online tool, and *Aligning Instruction to Standards: Just Ask Andie*, a quick reference guide available in hard copy and as an e-book. Teachers start with the standards and benchmarks, create learning targets and measures, and develop instructional activities that include instructing, demonstrating, and coaching students to learn.

Teachers start with developing a 30-Day Plan of learning targets and their measures. We recommend teachers use a 30-day increment because their minds can easily process the question, *What do I expect my students to be able to do in a particular subject area at the end of 30 days?* When teachers ask the same question using a semester time frame, it becomes difficult to visualize the plan and its breakdown.

So, teachers ask, what are the expectations for every 30 days and how does that break down into week one, week two, week three, and week four? For each 30-day span, teachers can answer the questions about their classroom practices as they analyze student learning results. For instance:

- What are our top priorities?
- How do we weight them?
- Which things should we stop doing or do less of?
- What do we do with students who are not hitting these targets?

Top priorities should include mastering the 10 to 15 common skills provided in the standards. Teachers use these priorities to create learning targets that build on each other to help students achieve the final results. Teachers also need to determine the weight of the measures that go into calculating the final result within a given time period, which usually translates into a letter grade. When teachers do these things, they immediately discover which of their actions are hindering rather than helping their students learn.

As Collins discovered in his work with companies and Studer discovered in his work with healthcare organizations, it is just as important for individuals to make a decision to stop doing those things that lead to negative results as it is for them to make a decision to put in place tactics that get results.

State content standards provide the foundation for establishing and communicating classroom learning targets that lead to desired student learning results. The school leader needs to make sure that teachers are aligning their instruction to the state standards and, if applicable, the district scope and sequence of the standards in each grade level. Teachers who create 30-Day Plans provide a "big picture" of learning targets that build on each other and align to state content standards. We realize that teachers may face limitations when school and district policies go against evidence-based classroom learning practices. In such cases, we hope school leaders will revisit their policies and align them more to what we know works and does not work when trying to achieve student learning results.

How to Apply Tactic 8

In compliance-driven classrooms, teachers tend to provide notations in their plan books that represent the content they will cover or the instructional activity they will use. However, lesson plan book notations seldom provide learning targets, measures, daily results, or the strategies teachers will use to help their students achieve the targets.

For teachers to know what to do from one day to the next, they need to know how well students accomplished the learning targets for the day and how much progress they are making toward achieving the final 30-day learning target. We have discovered that teachers have greater success with what and how well their students are learning when they sequence their learning targets and increase measurable expectations as students hit each one.

Remember the "sticky ball" example? The expectation or measure was increased gradually as students got better at throwing the sticky ball at the bull's-eye. The individuals were motivated to continue to practice because they knew they were trying to achieve 80 percent accuracy when they threw the ball 25 times.

"Chunking" Instruction

A prerequisite for putting in place a 30-Day Plan is for teachers to understand how to "chunk" instruction using learning targets and measures. Please refer to two resources, Figure 7.1 (taxonomy chart) and Figure 7.2 (scale of measures), as we demonstrate what we mean by "chunking" instruction.

In our example in Chapter 7, students were given several prompts and asked to write a well-organized paragraph. The teacher told them that they would be assessed on a 5-point scale based on the specific characteristics of a well-organized paragraph. Notice that the areas of assessment *do not* include correct grammar and spelling. Therefore, students will be assessed *only* on organization. They can demonstrate organization without using correct spelling and grammar in their writing. If a teacher marks them down for poor spelling and grammar when that was not communicated as an expectation, students will begin to lose learning momentum. The miscommunication breaks the level of trust between teacher and student.

Assessing organization only does not mean that it's not important to write with good spelling and grammar. If a teacher wants to teach, demonstrate, and practice with students how to write with proper spelling and grammar as students are creating a well-organized paragraph, the teacher needs to describe the characteristics of doing so and show how they are going to be measured.

One word of caution: Collins discovered when companies moved from good to great and stayed great, they did so when they had a Big Hairy Audacious Goal, or what he calls a BHAG, pronounced bee-hag. He defines a BHAG as a daunting goal that is clear and compelling and that people get right away. When teachers want students to get learning results, they need to create BHAGs and provide the right instruction and coaching that will help their students achieve them.

If the BHAG is for students to demonstrate that they can write a well-organized paragraph, then their focus turns to that one skill. Two students could write a well- organized paragraph and receive a perfect "5." One of the two may have better spelling and grammar in her writing. But because the BHAG's focus is on the paragraph's organization, the students would both receive a final score of "5" that translates into an "A" grade for that skill. The teacher now knows that she needs to work with the one student on spelling and grammar, but she does not penalize her for a measure that was not stated as being part of the evaluation.

At the end of the grading period various BHAGs will be included in a final grade. Every student will have a chance to master one BHAG at a time as she tries to achieve her best score for the final evaluation in which multiple categories will be assessed.

As indicated in Figure 7.2, the characteristics for writing a well-organized paragraph include the following:

- The paragraph has an introduction that gives the reader an indication of what the paragraph is going to be about.
- The conclusion leaves the reader with a sense of closure about the thoughts in the paragraph.
- Sequencing of thoughts is logical and effectively helps the reader know what the writer is describing.
- Transitions clearly connect one thought to another.

When chunking instruction in this instance, a teacher needs to make sure that students know what it takes to demonstrate the four characteristics above for writing a good paragraph. Each expectation should be broken down into instructional blocks. Figure 8.1 breaks down the first characteristic. The measurable learning targets show what students need to do to master each step in order to achieve the next. They act as building blocks that help the teacher know how to move from place to place in her instruction. Study the figure to see how the evaluated characteristics are broken down into defined measurable learning targets with measures for each target. This figure guides the teacher's instruction each day.

Figure 8.1. Learning Targets and Measures for Writing a Good Introduction

Evaluated Characteristic	Measurable Learning Targets	Measures
The paragraph has an introduction that gives the reader an indication of what the paragraph is going to be about.	• Identify characteristics of a good introduction. • Describe what students need to do to write a good introduction to a paragraph. • Given two paragraphs, choose the one that has a good introduction. • Explain why one paragraph has a good introduction and one does not. • Take a paragraph with a poor introduction and rewrite it so that it has a good introduction.	• 100% students raise green card on final assessment • 100% students raise green card on final assessment • Given 10 examples of 2 paragraphs, students select 9 out of 10 correctly. • 100% students raise green card on final assessment • Given 5 poor introductions, rewrite 4 of 5 introductions correctly

For an example of how a teacher effectively scaffolds learning targets and chunks instruction, let's live the life of Ms. James. On the first day of a unit of instruction, she begins teaching her students how to "write a well-organized paragraph." Ms. James uses the characteristics above and the scale in Figure 7.2 to explain the overall learning target the students will achieve. She then tells students that they will start by demonstrating that they can write a good introduction to a paragraph.

She shows them the characteristics and the measures in Figure 8.1 that communicate the learning targets for writing a good introduction. Ms. James posts the chart (Figure 8.1) on the board every day beside the scale for writing a well-organized paragraph (Figure 7.2). These two diagrams help students connect the dots. Students can see that they are learning the first of four evaluated characteristics for writing a well-organized paragraph. They also see the specific learning targets and the expected measures for the first characteristic, writing a good introduction.

Ms. James's class represents the first time her students will be exposed to writing a well-organized paragraph. She lets them know that when the final evaluation is given she expects them to achieve at least a 4.0 on a 5-point scale. Students scoring a 4.0 or above will receive an "A," the highest grade possible.

Ms. James tells her students that they will be working each day to achieve one learning target at a time. She begins with the first learning target, "Identify characteristics of a good introduction." She teaches them about the characteristics. She puts a list on the board and asks them to determine if these items represent good or bad characteristics of introductions. She then asks them to describe in their own words on a sheet of paper what students need to do to create a good introduction to a paragraph.

Next, Ms. James asks them to read the information to their student groups and for the group members to select the one they think is most accurate. She asks someone in the group to read the one selected. She corrects any wrong information presented. As the information from the group is being read, she asks students to write down anything that is missing. If another group covers that item during the group presentations, they strike the item off their list.

Ms. James asks them to return to their groups and compare the lists that they believe the groups did not cover. A representative reports for the group. After each group presents, she asks the students to raise a green card if they agree with the group, red if they disagree, and yellow if they are unsure. Ms. James again corrects any wrong information presented. If Ms. James notes a missing item that no group recognized, she will call that to their attention and re-teach and demonstrate the item.

At the end of the day, Ms. James sends three lists of items home with the students and asks them to select the list that shows the characteristics for writing a good introduction. She also asks them to write an explanation for why they made the selection they did.

When they return the next day, she asks them to get out a clean sheet of paper and write a list of characteristics that a paragraph with a good introduction would have. When they finish, she asks them to retrieve their homework, which includes the list of characteristics they selected and their explanation for selecting the list. She asks them to compare the list they've just written with the list they selected on their homework assignment.

Ms. James gives them the correct answers to the homework and asks them once again to compare their list to the correct one. She then asks for students to raise a green card if they have learned the target, yellow if they are not sure, and red if they still do not know how to achieve the target. As indicated in Figure 8.1, she expects 100 percent of the students to achieve the first two learning targets. If the majority of the students have not achieved it, she continues with the target. If a few students have not achieved it, she moves on and does extra work with those who continue to need help on the target.

Ms. James's ability to "chunk" instruction reinforces what Harry Wong tells us when he speaks about the value of making sure that teachers have well-managed classrooms. Wong reinforces that when students are doing work, they are learning. Those not working are not learning. In this example, the students participate because the learning target is clear. They see what needs to be done in order to identify characteristics of a good introduction. They see what they need to do to write a good introduction. They see that their classwork and homework have purpose and meaning.

The teacher will spend several days working with students on writing good introductions. Once she completes the instruction based on the measurable learning targets and gets a measure of her students' progress, she moves to the second characteristic for writing a well-organized paragraph, "The conclusion leaves the reader with a sense of closure about the thoughts in the paragraph." She can apply her outcomes and processes now to writing good conclusions.

A teacher's goal is for her students to learn and to sustain what they have learned over time. When Ms. James completes this instructional unit on writing well-organized paragraphs, students will be able to apply that knowledge when they are asked to complete writing assignments in their other classes and on the standardized, end-of-the-year writing assessment.

To create 30-Day Plans teachers must first understand how to sequence learning targets and chunk instruction. They then can put a plan together with standards, learning targets, and measures. Not properly sequencing learning targets and chunking instruction makes it difficult for students to achieve the 30-day learning results expected.

30-Day Plans

Now, let's look at some examples of how teachers "chunk" or scaffold instruction to create 30-Day Plans. These plans can be shared with students and their parents. A 30- Day Plan includes the 30-day learning target, the weekly learning targets, the day-to-day assessments, and the weekly assessments. Teachers use the 30-Day Plan to create a blueprint or a road map for daily learning targets and as a way to coach students and assess learning. When teachers create such plans, students come to class each day knowing what they are expected to do.

In contrast to performance-driven classrooms, teachers in compliance-driven classrooms tend to teach a "fun" activity or assign a worksheet for students to complete and then select state benchmarks that they believe the activity covers. Some teachers also use packaged curriculum and assessments and provide students with daily external rewards in hopes of motivating them to learn. Teachers use trinkets, candy, toy boxes, and even grades as prizes to bribe students to do work. The result is that students focus more on getting the prize rather than on achieving well-defined and communicated targets and measures.

Teachers, students, and parents have better experiences in performance-driven classrooms where teachers align and communicate goals, behaviors, and procedures. Students like to succeed, and when they experience success, they become more eager to learn. In performance-driven classrooms where teachers use 30-Day Plans, students have opportunities to succeed every day.

Mae MacDonald and Hope VanAmburg are first grade teachers at Spencer Bibbs Elementary School in Pensacola, Florida. They worked together to create a 30-Day Plan, as seen in Figure 8.2, for their first 30 days of school. They set three 30-day learning targets.

First, students identified rules and procedures for the class. Next, they demonstrated the rules and procedures for the class. Third, at the end of 30 days, students demonstrated improved proficiency in fluency. Ms. MacDonald and Ms. VanAmburg assessed the students during the first week so that they could chart their improvement in fluency each week. They expected all students to show improvement from where they began in week one. These teachers created their weekly plans by including daily learning targets and assessments using the 30-Day Plan in Figure 8.2.

Figure 8.2. 30-Day Plan

30-DAY PLAN	
Date for Plan Implementation:	
30-Day Learning Targets: • Identify appropriate classroom rules and procedures. • Demonstrate appropriate classroom rules and procedures. • Demonstrate improved proficiency in fluency.	
Week One	
Weekly Learning Targets	Identify appropriate classroom rules and procedures. Demonstrate classroom rules and procedures. Perform on a diagnostic literacy assessment for fluency.
Weekly Assessments	Paper and pencil test read to students using happy and sad faces Passage on a late kindergarten level from A – Z books
Week Two	
Weekly Learning Targets	Continue rules and procedures if not mastered. Recognize the difference between fluent and non-fluent reading.
Weekly Assessments	Teacher developed "Fluent and Non-Fluent Reading Assessment"
Week Three	
Weekly Learning Targets	Continue rules and procedures if not mastered. Imitate fluent readers.
Weekly Assessments	Teacher developed "Fluent Reading Performance Assessment"
Week Four	
Weekly Learning Targets	Continue rules and procedures if not mastered. Demonstrate repeated timed reading.
Weekly Assessments	A – Z passages at the same level as the passages used during the week

© Janet K. Pilcher

Also, they used the 30-Day Plan to create four weekly plans that included weekly learning targets. During the process they answered the following questions:

- What will students need to know and be able to do to achieve the weekly learning targets? (Daily learning targets written in measurable terms)
- What will I do this week to help students achieve the daily learning targets so that students can achieve the weekly learning targets?

- How will I know if students achieve the daily learning targets so that students can achieve the weekly learning targets?
- How will I communicate progress on the learning targets to students each day?

Figure 8.3 provides an example of the weekly plan for the second week of instruction guided by the 30-Day Plan. Ms. MacDonald and Ms. VanAmburg created the weekly plan to align to the week two literacy learning target, "Recognize the difference between fluent and non-fluent reading."

Figure 8.3. Sample Weekly Instructional Plan Aligned to 30-Day Plan

Weekly Learning Target for Week Two
Recognize the difference between fluent and non-fluent reading.

What will students need to know and be able to do to achieve the weekly learning targets? (*Daily learning targets written in measurable terms*)   • Students will define fluency.   • Students will recognize fluent reading from recorded passages.   • Students will list characteristics of fluent reading.   • Students will recognize non-fluent reading from recorded passages.   • Students will list characteristics of non-fluent reading.   • Students will distinguish between fluent and non-fluent reading when listening to recorded passages.
What will I do this week to help students achieve the daily learning targets so that students can achieve the weekly learning targets?   • I will define fluency by explaining to children the three principles that make a reader fluent (prosody, speed, accuracy). This will be done in "kid-friendly" terms.   • I will provide examples and non-examples of recorded passages for students to list characteristics of each.   • As a class, we will create a T-chart comparing fluent reading to non-fluent reading.
How will I know if students achieve the daily learning targets so that students can achieve the weekly learning targets?   • I will give a formative assessment using thumbs up for fluent reading and thumbs down for non-fluent reading. This will be done by the teacher reading a passage, or by the children listening to a recorded passage.   • At the end of the week, students will take a summative assessment. Students will distinguish fluent and non-fluent reading by circling a happy face or sad face. This will be done by the teacher reading a passage, or by the children listening to a recorded passage.
How will I communicate progress on the learning targets to students each day?   • Each day the students will be given examples of each. While the students are giving thumbs up or down during the formative assessment, I will give immediate feedback to them. We will also review the summative assessment at the end of the week, explaining why each passage was fluent or non-fluent reading.

© Janet K. Pilcher

The example provided by the two first grade teachers demonstrates how instruction scaffolds from week to week and day to day. Chunking instruction in this way allows teachers to help students connect the dots in order to achieve the 30-day student learning results. Students are not judged by being given a grade while they are practicing. Rather, the teacher assigns a final grade or score on the weekly summative assessments and the overall 30-day assessment.

When school leaders help teachers create and follow 30-Day Plans, both students and parents clearly understand what students are learning each week of a given month. In addition, school leaders can review a teacher's 30-Day Plan to determine what students are learning and when learning is occurring. This information is much more beneficial than one or two sentences in a teacher's lesson plan book on a given day.

What a Teacher Says About 30-Day Plans

"Learning how to create and apply a 30-Day Plan was one of the most important things I learned. I need to think about what students need to learn and in what sequence rather than starting with what I am going to teach. When I applied the 30-Day Plan in my class, I noticed that my students were more involved in what they were trying to accomplish."

(Response on the final evaluation from a teacher who completed the Teachers Teach, Students Learn Academy*)*

CHAPTER

Tactic 9:
Coach Teachers on How to Appropriately Assign Grades

Why Tactic 9 Is Important

In the late '80s Rick Stiggins, David Frisbie, and Phillip Griswold conducted a study, *Inside High School Grading Practices*, which observed the grading practices of high school teachers. In the study they said that though researchers had spent 20 to 25 years studying grading practices, little empirical evidence was available to help teachers understand what works, what doesn't work, and what should work. The study influenced Janet to conduct research in the early '90s using one of the recommendations Stiggins, Frisbie, and Griswold offered at the end of their study findings. In her study, students', teachers', and parents' perceptions of what grades mean were studied. She found that each of the three audiences interpreted the meaning of the grades differently.

Similar to this study, over the last several decades, scholars have followed up with studies on grading practices and continuously discover that individuals assign different meanings to grades. Unfortunately, research that shows what works and presents best practices in how to appropriately assign grades is not followed in schools and districts. As was stated in the article written by Stiggins and his colleagues, much of the basis for grading comes from folklore or traditions teachers experienced themselves. This still holds true in today's classrooms.

The initial findings from the Stiggins, Frisbie, and Griswold study and other research data from the past several decades show which practices help students learn and which practices hinder students from becoming engaged in their own learning. The studies show that teachers should assign grades on demonstrated performance of learning targets only after they have given their students an opportunity to practice the skill, make mistakes, correct their mistakes, and receive specific feedback on how to achieve the measures. When teachers assign grades while students are still practicing the skill, they are expecting their students to be perfect. This, as we previously mentioned, sets students up for failure. The reality is that the greatest opportunities for learning occur when students make mistakes, evaluate their mistakes, and take corrective action.

Second, as we suggested in Chapter 8, teachers should clearly communicate to students their scoring plan, measures, weights, and method for calculating grades. When students can see what they need to accomplish to receive a particular score or grade, they come to class each day prepared to learn. Teachers do not have to motivate them to do their work. Students understand the expectations, the measures, and the steps they need to complete in order to receive a good grade. Eventually, they begin to gain passion for achieving the learning targets and see that their work is worthwhile. And of course, they are learning every step of the way.

At the end of the grading period, the overall learning targets and the weights attached to them determine a student's grade. The grade needs to be representative of how well the student learned each skill. But it will also be affected by the weight given to each learning target. Remember, grades have been assigned well when they reflect the overall level of learning for the student.

Lastly, factors that reflect behaviors or represent a failure to follow rules or procedures should not be included in the grade. The grade should reflect only what the student has or hasn't learned. As we learned from Harry Wong, classrooms should have rules and those rules should have consequences. Students who choose to break rules are subject to the consequences in the discipline plan. The behavioral consequences should not get mixed up in their grade, which is an indicator of their learning achievement. If behavioral consequences are mixed into a student's grade, it can no longer be looked at as an indicator of the measures in the 30-Day Plan.

For example, when a student fails to complete a homework assignment, she could be violating a general rule, "Be prepared for class every day." Instead of receiving a "zero" on the assignment, which is never an acceptable grading practice, she should face the system of consequences that the teacher taught during the first week of school and that has been reinforced every week. Conversely, those students who did complete the homework assignment should not receive a completion grade simply for doing the work. They should receive the grade that reflects how well they achieved the learning target as defined by the measure.

How to Apply Tactic 9

In our work with teachers, we've found that school leaders and teachers prefer to use the concept of the 30-Day Plan differently. For example, we usually work with teachers to create 30-Day Plans that align to approximately 20 days of instructional time (five working days a week). On the other hand, some school leaders prefer to review plans every six weeks or 30 full working days. Either works fine as long as the leader communicates his expectations and coaches teachers on those expectations.

In Figures 9.1 through 9.4, we provide a teaching strategy that a team of sixth grade teachers used to assign and record student data. The example includes the "chunked" learning targets that their students practiced and the weekly learning targets and measures that were used to assign grades to students. The weekly plans of the 30-Day Data Blueprint provided a road map that the teachers used to plan, deliver, and guide their instruction. As shown for the given 30-day time period, the sixth grade team focused on the state standard, "Develop an understanding of and fluency with multiplication and division of fractions."

Figure 9.1. Sample Week One 30-Day Data Blueprint

30-Day Data Blueprint Sixth Grade Math Class			
State Standard: Develop an understanding of and fluency with multiplication and division of fractions.			
30-Day Learning Target: Given number and word problems, solve by multiplying and dividing fractions giving the answer in the simplest fraction.			
30-Day Test: Given 40 problems, demonstrate mastery of overall weekly learning targets.			
Learning Targets	Measures	Timeline	Instructional Activity
• Identify the numerator and the denominator of a fraction.	10 out of 10	Day 1	
• Describe what it means to simplify fractions.	100% green cards	Day 1	
• Determine all the numbers that will divide into the numerator and the denominator.	9 out of 10	Day 2	
• Define the greatest common factor (GCF).	100% correctly written	Day 2	
• Given a list, choose the greatest common factor.	9 out of 10	Day 3	
Week One Learning Target: Given a fraction, apply the GCF to simplify the fraction	Grading Scale and Test Blueprint	Day 4	

© Janet K. Pilcher

Figure 9.2. Sample Week Two 30-Day Data Blueprint

30-Day Data Blueprint Sixth Grade Math Class			
State Standard: Develop an understanding of and fluency with multiplication and division of fractions.			
30-Day Learning Target: Given number and word problems, solve by multiplying and dividing fractions giving the answer in the simplest fraction.			
30-Day Test: Given 40 problems, demonstrate mastery of overall weekly learning targets.			
Learning Targets	Measures	Timeline	Instructional Activity
• Simplify each fraction.	10 out of 10	Day 5	
• List the steps for multiplying fractions.	100% correct	Day 5	
• Demonstrate how to multiply the numerator and denominator.	10 out of 10	Day 6	
• Demonstrate proficiency on weeks one and two targets.	20 out of 20	Day 7	
Week Two Learning Target: Given a problem, solve by multiplying and give the answer in the simplest fraction.	Grading Scale and Test Blueprint	Day 8	

Figure 9.3. Sample Week Three 30-Day Data Blueprint

30-Day Data Blueprint Sixth Grade Math Class			
State Standard: Develop an understanding of and fluency with multiplication and division of fractions.			
30-Day Learning Target: Given number and word problems, solve by multiplying and dividing fractions giving the answer in the simplest fraction.			
30-Day Test: Given 40 problems, demonstrate mastery of overall weekly learning targets.			
Learning Targets	Measures	Timeline	Instructional Activity
• List the steps for dividing fractions.	100% correct	Day 9	
• Explain the difference between the steps used to multiply and divide fractions.	100% correct	Day 9	
• Simplify each multiplied or divided fraction to the simplest fraction.	10 out of 10	Day 10	
• Apply the inversion rule to divide fractions.	10 out of 10	Day 10, 11	
• Demonstrate proficiency on weeks one, two, and three targets.	25 out of 25	Day 12	
Week Three Learning Target: Given a problem, solve by dividing and give the answer in the simplest fraction.	Grading Scale and Test Blueprint	Day 13	

© Janet K. Pilcher

Figure 9.4. Sample Week Four 30-Day Data Blueprint

30-Day Data Blueprint Sixth Grade Math Class			
State Standard: Develop an understanding of and fluency with multiplication and division of fractions.			
30-Day Learning Target: Given number and word problems, solve by multiplying and dividing fractions giving the answer in the simplest fraction.			
30-Day Test: Given 40 problems, demonstrate mastery of overall weekly learning targets.			
Learning Targets	Measures	Timeline	Instructional Activity
• When reading a word problem, re-state what the problem is asking.	5 out of 5	Day 14	
• Determine if the problem requires multiplication or division of fractions.	8 out of 10	Day 14	
• Given word problems with answers, analyze if the answer seems like a reasonable answer.	9 out of 10	Day 15	
• Given a word problem, solve by multiplying or dividing and giving the answer in the simplest fraction.	9 out of 10	Day 16, 17	
• Re-read the worked problem and analyze if your answer seems like a reasonable solution.	9 out of 10	Day 16, 17	
• Demonstrate proficiency on weeks one, two, three, and four targets.	20 out of 25	Day 18	
Week Four Learning Target: Given a word problem, solve by multiplying or dividing, and give the answer in the simplest fraction.	Grading Scale and Test Blueprint	Day 19	
Close Learning Gaps on all Targets	32 out of 35	Day 20	
30-Day Test	Grading Scale and Test Blueprint	Day 21	

The sixth grade math team first created the 30-day learning target to show that students would be responsible for multiplying and dividing fractions when working number and word problems. They then created shorter-term learning targets aimed at helping students achieve the 30-day learning target.

Remember that instruction on the weekly learning targets may not last all five days, or it may last longer. The term "week" is used loosely. Some weekly learning targets might take three days of instructional time for students to achieve them while others might take seven or eight days.

Next, the team created lessons for the weekly learning targets that aligned with the 30-day learning target. As you see, they chunked their instruction by sequencing learning targets for each week. Each teacher on the team created different instructional activities for students, but they all worked together to create the 30-day learning target, the weekly learning targets, the daily sequenced targets, and the measures. The teachers made sure that students achieved the measures for each sequenced learning target before they assessed them for the purpose of assigning a grade.

The measures associated with the sequenced learning targets were not used to grade students. Once students had time to practice and achieve the measures for each learning target, the team gave a lesson test and determined how well students had achieved the weekly learning targets. The scores on the lesson tests were included in a student's final grade based on the grading scale provided by the teacher. At the end of the 30-day period, students practiced all skills at once before taking the final 30-day test.

Finally, the teachers gave the 30-day test and recorded the achievement levels of their students. The numbers of the problems for the 30-day test were included in a 30-day test blueprint that included the learning targets, number of problems for each target, and the number of points for each item. The teachers were able to look at the missed problems on the 30-day test to determine where students were excelling and where, if any place, they needed more assistance.

To analyze how well their students learned the material, the teachers needed to find a meaningful and organized way to record the weekly test scores and the 30-day test score. As seen in Figure 9.5, they created a spreadsheet that reflected the information. The spreadsheet shows each student's results for the four weekly learning targets indicated by the summative weekly tests and the 30-day test score. The spreadsheet allowed the teachers to use the data to create class data charts that indicated where they should modify their instruction in order to get better student learning results, and that allowed them to share information with others on how well the class performed on the 30-day goal in a given content area.

Figure 9.5. Sample 30-Day Student Results Data Report

30-Day Student Results Data Report					
State Standard/Benchmark: Develop an understanding of and fluency with multiplication and division of fractions.					
30-Day Learning Target: Given a number or word problem, solve by multiplying or dividing and giving the answer in the simplest fraction.					
Overall Weekly Learning Targets	**Measure**	**Weight**	**Score**	**Student 1**	**Student 2**
Given a fraction, apply the GCF to simplify the fraction.	Weekly score = 20 problems End of unit score = 10 problems	0.5 1.0	10 possible 10 possible Total possible = 20	8 10 18	7 10 17
Given a problem, solve by multiplying and giving the answer in the simplest fraction.	Weekly score = 20 problems End of unit score = 10 problems	0.5 2.0	10 possible 20 possible Total possible = 30	9 20 29	8 18 26
Given a problem, solve by dividing and giving the answer in the simplest fraction.	Weekly score = 20 problems End of unit score = 10 problems	0.5 2.0	10 possible 20 possible Total possible = 30	10 20 30	9 20 29
Given a word problem, evaluate it by multiplying or dividing fractions.	Weekly score = 10 problems End of unit score = 10 problems	1.0 2.0	10 possible 20 possible Total possible = 30	9 20 29	7 18 25
			Total possible = 110	106	97
SCALE: 99 – 110 points = Strong A 86 – 98 points = Effective B 77 – 85 points = Developing C 67 – 76 points = Needs Help D Below 67 points = Danger Zone F					
Student Behavior in 30 Days for Breaking Rules				0	One 1st level Two 2nd level
Parent Satisfaction Score on Overall Satisfaction Rating				5	5

© Janet K. Pilcher

As shown in Figure 9.5, the sixth grade team organized their data by a state standard, the 30-day learning target, and the breakdown of the weekly learning targets that students needed to achieve in order to master the 30-day learning target. The measures and weights for the final weekly test and the end of unit or 30-day score were included. And the report also included documentation of the consequences received by students for breaking the rules and a parent satisfaction rating by each student's parents.

Students were assessed by the teacher on each weekly target as soon as the instruction had been given, students were given a chance to practice, and teachers coached students to learn. Each student was given a score on each weekly learning target and a second score on the overall weekly target, which is reflected by the final 30-day test score.

The final grade needs to reflect how well students have achieved the overall targets aligned with the 30-day learning target. The final assessment represents the most current measure of what students have and have not achieved. For example, look at the final score of student 2. When you add the lesson tests and unit test score, you'll see he has a total score of 97. As he practiced throughout the month, he clearly improved on simplifying fractions. During the first week, he performed 14 out of 20 problems correctly on the end-of-week test. On the final 30-day test, he correctly answered 10 out of 10 problems on that same skill.

The first end-of-week test score makes the final grade the student receives a borderline case. Had he scored 99 rather than 97 points, the student would have received a final grade of an "A" for the unit of instruction. In this circumstance and other borderline grade assignment cases, extra credit serves a meaningful purpose. The teacher could give the student 10 simplification problems and replace the score of 7 with the new score. If the student demonstrates mastery by getting 9 or 10 problems correct, the final score changes to better reflect the current level of mastery. The student then receives an "A," representing his level of achievement on the 30-day goal.

The team of sixth grade teachers assigned grades using the data gathered for each student over a 30-day period. As shown in Figure 9.5, teachers recorded five scores for each student—four weekly test scores and a 30-day test score—which they used to assign grades. A student's grade represented as accurately as possible his level of achievement on the 30-day learning target. Teachers, students, and parents should be able to look at the final grade for any given 30-day learning target and trust that the grade represents the level of student mastery for the weekly learning targets aligned with the 30-day learning target.

When students have been successfully taught by teachers using sequenced learning targets, they will be able to sustain their learning and achieve a high score on end-of-year standardized tests aligned with state standards. Continuing the current common practice of having students take practice tests over and over again does not help them achieve sustainable gains on standardized tests each year. Rather, students are simply complying with the requirements rather than valuing what they are learning.

Likewise, students of teachers who develop and apply 30-Day Plans and record student learning results have better opportunities to achieve sustainable learning gains. Students know what is expected of them and know how their learning will be measured.

Because they require that teachers stop doing things they have done for years, Tactics 8 and 9 may seem to be some of the hardest for teachers to put in place. Still, making the effort is worth it. Once teachers make the leap and see the strides their students are making, they will be glad they did.

These tactics require that teachers create systematic and organized ways to record student learning data. Each teacher should create the system of recording student learning data on daily, weekly, and 30-day learning targets that works best for her. In this section, we provide an example of a 30-Day Plan used by a team of sixth grade teachers and the data reporting system they used to report the overall weekly and 30-day student learning results for each of their students.

School leaders must clearly understand Tactics 7, 8, and 9 so that they can coach and support teachers to shift from compliance- to performance-driven classrooms. Teachers in performance-driven classrooms know that what they measure, their students value. Teachers who continue compliance-driven practices to plan, deliver, and assess students jeopardize student learning.

Creating effective classrooms where students are not losing years of learning is hard work, especially when teachers must learn to shift from compliance-driven to performance-driven classrooms. There is no question that school leaders will have to work very hard to help teachers make the shifts needed to apply Principle 3.

School leaders must remember that in performance-driven classrooms, teachers lead students as they are learning and ultimately are the ones account-able for their students' achievement levels. When teachers have to make chang-es in their behaviors to try to get the flywheel moving, the work is difficult. But, remember what happens to the flywheel once student momentum begins to build. It moves so fast it seems unstoppable. Teachers then live their dreams of having purpose, doing worthwhile work, and making a difference in the lives of their students. Great teachers know that students will be more eager to learn when they clearly understand their learning targets and how they will be assessed on each one.

Tactics 7-9:
What Teachers Measure, Students Value

To achieve student learning and parent satisfaction results, school leaders must coach and support teachers to:

- Focus on student learning results rather than covering subject matter.

- Develop learning targets with measures that determine what students need to do in order to achieve.

- Develop learning targets that include a measurable capability verb from the taxonomy chart and a description of what a student will do to demonstrate performance and achieve results.

- Use daily learning targets and measures to determine how students will be assessed when they have had every opportunity to learn.

- Coach students to use the learning targets and measures to guide them each day on what they are supposed to learn and achieve.

- Use the learning targets and measures as a guide to determine what is taught each day.

- Analyze state standards/benchmarks to determine common knowledge and skills within the standards.

- Create learning targets with measures, chunk instruction by creating daily learning targets with guided measures, and grade students after they have been taught and have practiced hitting one learning target at a time.

- Create 30-Day Plans that include the 30-day learning target and the 30-day measure.

- Determine 30-day learning targets in subject areas and decide what students need to know and do in week one, week two, week three, and week four in order to hit the 30-day learning target.

- Assign grades for the "weekly" targets that align with the 30-day target and at the end of a 30-day time period. Grades are not assigned to students when they are being coached by the teacher or while they are still practicing to hit the targets.

- NOT use grades to punish or discipline students or to reward non-achievement factors.

- Create data reporting systems to record student assessment information on the weekly and 30-day learning targets. These data communicate achievement information to teachers, students, and parents. Other factors, including student behavior, are reported separately.

Principle 4:
When Teachers Coach, Students Learn

Studer recommends that when leaders are trying to help middle performing employees become high performing ones, they must support them, coach them, and then provide more support. Likewise, when teachers are coaching students, they are helping students improve their knowledge, skills, and performance in order to achieve well-defined learning targets.

Coaching is part of the teacher's job. A coach is a leader. A coach strategically and carefully analyzes and monitors the situation and uses her unique skills and experiences to guide students to achieve learning targets. Teachers acting as coaches partner with their students to help them align their goals with desired behaviors, communicate and clarify goals, and assess and support achievement of desired outcomes. Teacher coaches guide students to connect their purpose for learning with their desire to achieve success.

Sometimes studying the practices and philosophies of other types of coaches can be instructive for teachers. John Wooden, for example, is one of the greatest coaches of all time. His UCLA basketball teams won 10 NCAA championships. He coached some of the best players in the world. If you were to ask Coach Wooden who he believes is one of the best players he ever coached, you'd expect to hear names like Kareem Abdul-Jabbar or Bill Walton. But Coach Wooden has said in past interviews that Swen Nater is one of the greatest players he ever coached.

Nater was cut from his high school basketball team. Not giving up, he made a community college team and became talented enough that some small colleges offered him scholarships to play. UCLA expressed interest, too. At the time, Coach Wooden's teams had won seven out of the last eight national championships, Bill Walton was entering UCLA as the new center, and Nater was trying to figure out his next step after community college.

Coach Wooden met with Nater and had an honest conversation with him. He told Nater that he could go to a small school and play all the minutes he wanted to play, or he could come to UCLA, where he would never start a game, but where he could back up the greatest center in the country every day. Nater eagerly accepted, and just as Coach Wooden warned, he never started a game at UCLA.

Coach Wooden made it clear that Nater's job was to help Walton get better and better. He taught Nater about the game, coached him through mistakes, and practiced Nater with Walton every day. Someone once asked Walton to name the best center he had ever played against. Walton replied, "Swen Nater."

Nater won three championship rings in his time at UCLA. After leaving the school, he made history by becoming the first player who had never started in a college game to be selected in the first round of a professional draft. He went on to win several awards during his professional career.

Nater once recalled a time when he was frustrated about not playing. Coach Wooden invited him into his office to talk. As he unloaded his frustrations while expressing how much he wanted to learn and get better at his position, Nater expected to get a tough talk from Coach Wooden. But instead Coach Wooden listened intently, empathetically, and with great understanding. Nater says that for that half-hour Coach Wooden made him feel like he was the most important person in the world.

On the court, Coach Wooden now had even higher expectations of Nater, but he met those expectations. He knew that Coach Wooden cared about him and cared about making him the best player he could be, even if his main role was to help make Bill Walton the best center of all time.

Nater wrote a book with Ronald Gallimore about Coach Wooden's teaching principles and practices. They named the book after one of Coach Wooden's popular sayings, *You Haven't Taught Until Students Have Learned*. John Wooden was a great coach because he was a great teacher. He took what he learned on the court and transferred those principles into teaching. The book about Coach Wooden's teaching principles and practices serves as one of the best resources for connecting coaching to effective teaching.

Coach Wooden recognized and rewarded success, and, like Studer, discovered that recognized behavior gets repeated. What we reward, we get more of. When teachers reward students for doing the right things—working to achieve the learning targets, exhibiting good behaviors, and following procedures—students continue to do the right things. In his chapters on creating rules and procedures, Harry Wong suggests that teachers will get students to follow the rules and procedures when they reward the correct behaviors. Students like to be rewarded and recognized. Remember, it takes three compliments to one criticism to get a positive response. Therefore, reward and recognition should be part of performance-driven classrooms every day.

When teachers provide feedback on student work (Tactic 10), they need to be specific with the feedback provided so the students know what they are doing well and where they need to improve. Giving a student a check or a "good job" comment simply for completing an assignment does not encourage the student to keep trying to improve her performance. Students need to know how close they are to achieving the measure and what specifically they need to practice to get better.

Teachers can also recognize good behavior with specific feedback. For example, a teacher might say to a student, "Thank you for respecting others by allowing them to finish what they were saying before you reacted to their comments."

In addition to Tactic 10, we introduce two other tactics school leaders can follow: Tactic 11, which covers how school leaders can coach and support teachers as they round for outcomes on students, and Tactic 12, which covers how school leaders can help teachers harvest student wins. Each day, students do things that deserve to be recognized and rewarded. When teachers harvest wins by recognizing progress and rewarding success, they gain insights about students that they can share with parents as they apply the "three compliments to one criticism" principle. In turn, teachers create good relationships with students and parents.

Tactic 10:
Coach and Support Teachers as They Give Specific Feedback on Learning

Why Tactic 10 Is Important

At the turn of the century, Paul Black and Dylan Wiliam analyzed over 250 studies and found powerful results that should guide what teachers do in their classrooms each day. The findings show evidence that performance-driven classrooms yield high student learning results. Students whose teachers provided specific feedback to them as they were learning achieved significant learning gains on standardized assessments. In fact, the highest learning gains occurred for those students labeled "lowest achieving."

In schools achieving these gains, teachers provided clear learning expectations and students used the specific teacher feedback to improve. Their study provides some of the best evidence supporting why teachers should apply Tactic 10. Similar to Marzano's findings on the importance of teacher effectiveness, we believe that Black and Wiliam present some of the most important findings for school leaders to consider when working with teachers.

Also important is a recent article by Jan Chappuis, who has worked closely with Stiggins. The article, "Using Student-Involved Assessment to Close the Achievement Gap," suggests that students must first consider themselves successful learners in order to gain confidence in their abilities to learn. When students receive specific feedback reinforcing what they are doing right and the teacher directs them to modify their mistakes in a supportive way, they believe learning is possible.

Stiggins and his colleagues have reinforced with leaders and teachers the need to engage students in the learning and assessment processes used in the classroom. In Appendix 1, we provide several articles and books by Stiggins and his colleagues that reinforce the need to engage students in their own learning. When discussing Tactic 10, we provide some suggestions on how teachers can provide specific learning-focused feedback.

How to Apply Tactic 10

In performance-driven classrooms, teachers come to class every day with a game plan. They clearly state the learning targets and measures, teach and demonstrate how to succeed, get students to practice, gather information to check on their progress, make any modifications necessary to close the learning gaps, and recognize success on specific learning, behavioral, and procedural accomplishments.

When providing instruction on the learning targets, Stiggins and Chappuis suggest several strategies that teachers can use to help students know where they are going. For example, they suggest teachers present strong and weak examples aligned with a particular learning target. Students must know what achieving at the highest level looks like. When reviewing the weak examples, students use assessment criteria provided by the teacher to reflect on how the work needs to be improved. Also, when teachers assign practice work to students either in class or as homework, students should recognize that the work helps them achieve the learning targets.

In our work in classrooms, we often hear students complain that teachers give them busy work in class and as homework to keep them occupied and quiet. It is also not uncommon for teachers to punish students who don't complete their work by assigning them a "zero." The Black and Wiliam study results and the evidence that Stiggins has collected from teachers over the past three decades tell us that students are more motivated to do homework and classwork when it aligns to the learning targets and measures that determine their level of success. This situation tells us punishments do not motivate students; rather, rewards from their successes do.

Some teachers tell us that providing specific feedback takes too much time and is not a realistic task to expect of them. However, when teachers use their creativity to determine various ways of collecting information from students, they'll see that it is possible for the task to take minimal effort.

Here are some examples for how teachers can provide descriptive feedback to students:

Self and Peer Assessment. Ms. James's students used green, yellow, and red cards to show their current level of learning with regard to a learning target. To give feedback to students, teachers can also use tools like the scale of measures provided in Figure 7.2. Recall that Ms. James created learning targets for each of the characteristics for writing a well-organized paragraph and used those targets to teach students how to demonstrate performance on each.

Using the scales and sequenced learning targets and their corresponding guided measures, her students were able to self-assess or assess each other's work while they were practicing a specific skill. One skill built on the other until eventually the students hit the final target. Ms. James provided feedback to students, students assessed their own progress, and students provided feedback to their peers using a common target and guided measure. Students used the descriptions and measures on the assessment guide for writing a well-organized paragraph to assess their progress.

Group Tests and Traffic Lighting. When we worked with high school mathematics teachers, we taught them how to use group tests. The teachers gave students three problems to work and asked them to first work the problems individually. Then, using specific procedures for forming groups, they formed groups of three and described to each other what they did to work the problems. The group then determined whether the problems in the group were correctly or incorrectly worked. Keeping with our red, yellow, and green theme, students held the card that represented their confidence level in getting each problem correct. The teachers gave students the correct answers and then asked again that they raise their green or red cards to indicate if they worked the problem correctly or not. This strategy gives teachers a quick way to determine how well students are doing on achieving the learning target.

Student Surveys. In our classes today, we use a survey at the end of each class to gather information from students. We analyze the information they give us and begin the class the next day by going over the results. This activity provides a great review from the prior day, and students enjoy receiving the feedback. Figure 10.1 provides the survey we use in our classes.

Figure 10.1 End-of-Class Survey

	Highly Agree	Agree	Neutral	Disagree	Highly Disagree
Did you learn something new today?	5	4	3	2	1
Did you value what you learned today?	5	4	3	2	1
Do you feel like you mastered the learning target(s)?	5	4	3	2	1
Do you have a good sense of where we are going next?	5	4	3	2	1
Are there learning gaps that are keeping you from achieving the learning target(s)?	5	4	3	2	1
What are the most important things you have learned today?					
What questions do you still have?					

© Janet K. Pilcher

Thumbs Up, Thumbs Down. When teaching classroom rules and procedures, Ms. MacDonald and Ms. VanAmburg used "thumbs up" and "thumbs down" with their first graders. As the teachers acted out a behavior, their students gave them a "thumbs up" if the behavior represented one that they should model and a "thumbs down" if not. This strategy works well with young children.

"Act On It NOW" Note. We have created "sticky" notes that teachers can place on student work. The teacher completes an "Act On It Now" note and then posts the note on the student work. Based on the information on the note, the student knows specifically what he did well and what he needs to do in order to improve his work.

ACT ON IT NOW!
To: Date: Assignment:
What you did well:
What could be improved:

© Janet K. Pilcher

These are just a few examples of the many possible strategies teachers can use to give students specific feedback on their work. Every one of them is much more valuable for students than a checkmark, a "good job," or a "needs improvement" placed on student work. Another positive is that students find descriptive feedback strategies fun and helpful.

Relying on the important Black and Wiliam study, school leaders can feel confident that when teachers coach students by providing descriptive feedback, they make it easier for their students to achieve benchmarked learning results. To do this well, school leaders need to coach teachers and support their efforts to gather information from students in order to get a sense of where students believe they are in the learning process.

The quality of the feedback teachers provide and retrieve moves students closer and closer to hitting their learning targets. Stiggins suggests that applying this tactic shifts the responsibility for learning from the teacher to the student. Students learn best when they take control of their own learning. Put another way, teachers may be the leaders in their classrooms, but students make the choice to learn, behave, and follow procedures.

11

Tactic 11:
Coach and Support Teachers as They Round for Outcomes on Students

Why Tactic 11 Is Important

Have you ever been a patient in a hospital and had your doctor stop by your room on her daily rounds? Do you remember what it felt like? You probably felt valued and your anxiety probably lessened because you knew she was concerned about your well-being. When teachers round on students in the classroom, they can have the same effect.

Great teachers walk into their classrooms every day deeply caring that all students experience success. John Wooden, one of the most successful teachers and coaches of all time, defined success as "peace of mind, which is a direct result of self-satisfaction in knowing you have made the effort to become the best you are capable of becoming." He believes that this definition holds true for every student who enters a classroom.

When all students are convinced to focus on their progress, Wooden says they gain and maintain motivation. Coach Wooden's basketball players knew that he cared about them. He created relationships with every single one of his players as he guided them to become successful. Teachers can do the same.

Studer's work with healthcare leaders shows us that rounding for outcomes helps leaders connect with and develop relationships with others. Rounding also provides a way for leaders to collect information that will help them determine what is and isn't going well and what employees need in order to do their jobs better. In their classrooms, teachers are the leaders. As the leaders, teachers round on students in order to develop relationships with and gather information from them.

In order for relationships to develop, specific acts of care must occur. Consistent practices help us connect to people each day. For teachers to connect with students in their classroom, we suggest that teachers round on their students. In Chapter 10, we provided ways that teachers can give feedback to their students on how well they are learning.

Rounding on students is different from providing feedback on their work. It does not focus directly on learning. Rather, when they round, teachers focus on making sure students are not experiencing things that are getting in the way of learning. Rounding also shows students that teachers care about them as individuals.

How to Apply Tactic 11

Studer proposes that leaders use four questions when rounding on their employees. Here we slightly modify his rounding questions so that teachers can use them with their students. We suggest that school leaders coach and support teachers as they round on students. Teachers should ask their students the following three questions:

- What is working well for you in class?
- Are there any individuals whom I should be recognizing?
- Is there anything keeping you from being successful in class?

As teachers are rounding on students, they record their answers in a rounding log similar to the one in Figure 11.1. Classrooms are different, especially at different grade levels. So teachers round using different strategies. Regardless of the strategies being used, however, teachers should prepare students for rounding. They need to create a procedure for rounding, teach the procedure, and have students practice the procedure. Taking these steps will keep rounding from being disruptive to classroom learning or to the teacher and student participating in the rounding.

Over time students will come to value rounding. Therefore, teachers can make rounding a sacred activity that requires the highest level of respect from others when it occurs in class. The consequences for breaking the rule "Respect others" when a teacher is rounding on students needs to be more severe than the day-to-day consequences for breaking the rule. Increasing the severity of the consequences tells students that the teacher highly values rounding and that she cares about their well-being and wants the rounding session to be productive for everyone.

As with rules and procedures, teachers must teach, demonstrate, and practice rounding on students so that students are very clear about what happens in class when rounding is occurring. Rounding conversations focus on what is occurring in the classroom that helps or hinders their learning.

If students address issues occurring outside of the classroom or that are indirectly related to the classroom learning environment, teachers need to refocus the conversation on the classroom and handle the other situation separately. To keep the conversations focused on learning, teachers need to teach students what they mean when they ask them to "keep the conversations focused on learning," and to demonstrate what productive conversations look like.

Figure 11.1 Student Rounding for Outcomes Log

Student Rounding for Outcomes Log			
Class:		Date:	
	What is working well for you in class?	Are there any individuals I should be recognizing?	Is there anything keeping you from being successful in class?
Name of Student			
Name of Student			
Name of Student			

Adapted with permission from Studer Group, 2001©

Teachers schedule rounding times with students. Depending on the number of students in a classroom and the time of the class period, teachers determine how often they can round on students. There are several effective ways to incorporate rounding into the period. For example, teachers can round when students are practicing their work individually. Or they can integrate rounding into instruction as students are participating with their peers in student learning centers. As students are working with other students completing the work in their centers, a teacher designates one as the rounding center. To not disrupt group work, students in the rounding center do individual work while the teacher meets with each student in a designated place. TAGOS Leadership Academy is a charter high school that uses student rounding in yet another way. High school students are assigned an advisor who rounds on students at appropriate times.

Rounding provides extremely useful information to teachers and makes students feel valued and, thus, more motivated to tackle their daily learning targets. Rounding connects teachers to students, makes students feel cared for, and puts the learning flywheel in motion.

TAGOS Leadership Academy

Curriculum for the TAGOS Leadership Academy located in Janesville, Wisconsin, consists of student-driven project-based learning experiences along with a self-directed computerized accelerated math program. Students complete research projects in a business-like setting based on their interests and passions. Students consult with their advisors to tailor-make a standards-based curriculum that meets individual student needs. Advisors meet with students to set and achieve project goals. The advisors round on the students to determine:

- What is working well
- Who needs to be recognized
- If students have the tools and equipment to learn in their project-based learning setting

For more information about the TAGOS Leadership Academy, please visit www.tagosleadershipacademy.org.

CHAPTER 12

Tactic 12:
Help Teachers Harvest Student Wins

Why Tactic 12 Is Important

Everyone likes to be recognized and rewarded when they do something good. And when our actions are rewarded, we repeat them. In compliance-driven classrooms students experience a common type of reward—grades. The students motivated by grades are usually those who have experienced some success with grades, who value the discipline required to do the work being graded, or who fear the consequences they'll face at home if certain grades are not reported.

Some students work to receive an "A." Others are satisfied with doing just enough work to pass. The reality is that when rewards are attached to grades, the meaning of the reward becomes very fuzzy. Parents reward students for achieving. Students interpret the reward as doing what it takes to get the desired grade. Many students in today's classrooms experience this set of events. And if you think back on your own experience as a student in school, you will most likely remember how you worked the classroom system to do what it took to get a desired grade.

As previously mentioned, in performance-driven classrooms, students focus on hitting learning targets with measures. This approach to learning is very different from the "Get rewarded with a good grade" system that occurs in compliance-driven classrooms.

One big advantage of performance-driven classrooms is that teachers have many opportunities to recognize the successes of students and in turn encourage them to repeat those successes and behaviors. Great teachers want to openly recognize what students are doing to move closer to achieving the learning targets. Recognizing and rewarding good work along the way motivates students to keep practicing until they reach the final goal.

Studer points out that many of us tend to feel uncomfortable when we compliment others. Or we get too wrapped up in the potential negative outcomes of recognizing and rewarding people. On page 216 of *Results That Last*, Studer describes possible beliefs and attitudes that could keep us from harvesting wins with others. Here are his six holdbacks, which we have modified slightly for classrooms:

- *Big Head*: "If I compliment them too much, they'll get a big head!"
- *Complacency*: "If I tell them they did a good job, they'll get complacent!"
- *Martyrdom*: "My teachers never complimented me; why should I compliment my students?"
- *Another Day, Another Dollar*: "They should just be happy that I didn't penalize them more than I did—in fact, they should be grateful they didn't get an F on that assignment!"
- *Scrooge Mentality*: "I can give only so many compliments a week!"
- *Pride*: "This is hokey!"

And we add one more to the list:

- *Fairness*: "It is impossible to do. I have to make sure everyone is treated the same."

In order to harvest wins, you'll have to lose these misconceptions.

Harvesting student wins requires that teachers do two things. First, teachers must commit to the practice of recognizing and rewarding good work. Second, they have to overcome any negative beliefs or attitudes they harbor about complimenting students.

Coach Wooden came up with an approach he labeled, "earned and deserved." In their book on Wooden's teaching style and practices, Nater and Gallimore present the following quote from him: "I believe in order to be fair to all students, teachers must give individual students the treatment they earn and deserve. The most unfair thing to do is to treat all of them the same."

When you put a plan into action that will help you harvest student wins, remember two things: 1) Recognized behavior gets repeated, and 2) It takes three compliments to one criticism to get positive results. Harvesting student wins is an essential tactic for teachers because it helps them keep the "learning flywheel" moving for every student.

How to Apply Tactic 12

Most people become more motivated when they receive a reward that aligns to their good performance, when they receive written and personal appreciation for a specific performance, or when they are openly praised in a public place for a specific performance.

To be most effective, the recognition and reward should include accolades for a specifically defined performance so that people know exactly what they did right and can repeat the behavior. Keeping this principle in mind, there are many ways for teachers to recognize their students.

Borrowing from Studer's recommended practices with some slight modifications to fit students in classrooms, using some examples from Toledo Blade Elementary School in Sarasota, Florida, and using some of our own, we provide examples for school leaders to use as they help teachers harvest wins with students.

Rounding. Part of rounding is asking the question, "Are there any individuals whom I should be recognizing?" At the end of every week or month, teachers could have a reward and recognition celebration based on the responses they received from their students to let the class know who recognized whom and for what action.

WOW Cards. Teachers could use WOW cards like the one presented below. During the week, the teacher distributes WOW cards to students who have achieved specific good actions and work. To further harvest the win, teachers could write a note home to the student's parents sharing the WOW card or she could give the parents a quick call.

WOW!! Card	Name: Class: Date:
TODAY YOU "WOWED" ME WHEN YOU	
Thank You!	Submitted by:

Adapted with permission from Studer Group, 2001 ©

Snack Bars with Kudos. Principal Chris Renouf encourages and supports teachers harvesting student wins in his school, Toledo Blade Elementary School, in Sarasota, Florida. He encourages his teachers to give out a snack bar along with a written message praising the student for a specific performance or behavior.

Difference Maker Highlighters. Students love highlighters, especially neat ones. Our staff at www.teacherready.net placed the saying, "I am a difference maker" on a three-pronged, multi-color highlighter. We recommend to teachers that when a student has been recognized by teachers or other students multiple times, give the student one of the "difference maker" highlighters. By giving the highlighter, teachers openly recognize a student's specific accomplishments in front of their peers.

Thank-You Notes. Studer is famous with many in the healthcare industry for his lessons on why it is important to hardwire thank-you notes in organizations. Thank-you notes have had an enormous impact on employee retention and satisfaction. Like the one below, they can be written by a teacher to let a student know when someone else has recognized him for a job well done. Or, they can be used when the teacher herself wants to recognize the student for something worthwhile or for a significant accomplishment. Teachers can also create a procedure that allows students to write thank-you notes to each other. (Keep in mind, though, teachers should always review student-to-student thank-you notes.) Studer recommends that thank-you notes be handwritten and that they focus on something specific the recipient has done.

THANK YOU!!!

Dear Justin,

Roger told me that he made a perfect score on his weekly test because you coached him to write a better introduction when writing a well-organized paragraph. You were a difference maker this week. Thank you, Justin.

Ms. Pilcher

30-Day Celebrations. To align with their 30-Day Plans, teachers can hold 30-day celebrations for students. These events celebrate class and individual accomplishments with regard to that 30-day period's learning targets and allow teachers to recognize the positive behaviors exhibited by their students. During these celebrations, high performers can be recognized as well as those students who've made significant improvements during the 30-day period. Remember that only students who have adequately or more than adequately performed and followed classroom rules and procedures should be recognized and rewarded. And the recognition should clearly connect to the behavior or performance being recognized.

Principal Renouf at Toledo Blade does something similar. He holds a school-wide celebration four times a year, each of which has a particular theme. All students and teachers participate in this celebration, which includes a rewards ceremony. Various students who are recognized invite their parents to the event. The students accept their awards from Principal Renouf. Only those who had exceptional performance or behavior participate in the awards ceremony. This type of praise motivates other students to improve their own performance.

School leaders should encourage teachers to think of many creative and fun ways to harvest student wins. When creating a system to harvest wins, teachers must be consistent and make sure that they are recognizing a very well-defined action each time. In our work with teachers, we have found that when they begin harvesting wins in their classrooms, their students' desire to perform becomes contagious.

By paying such close attention to what their students are achieving, teachers can begin to recognize the individual needs and differences of their students. Their students then see that their teachers value them, care about them, and want them to learn. In turn, teachers see that their work has purpose, is worthwhile, and that they are making a difference in their students' lives.

Tactics 10-12:
When Teachers Coach, Students Learn

To achieve student learning and parent satisfaction results, school leaders must coach and support teachers to:

- Take on a coaching role as they help students achieve their learning targets. Teachers should follow the principle that they have not taught well until students have learned.

- Create instructional and assessment strategies that involve students and provide very specific feedback to students in order to help them achieve the learning targets.

- Integrate formative assessment strategies that encourage students to take control of their own learning, or to become owners rather than renters of learning.

- Round on students to develop relationships with them and to find out if anything is keeping students from learning or wanting to learn.

- Develop a classroom procedure for rounding on students. During rounding sessions, ask students three questions:

- What is working well for you in class?
- Are there any individuals whom I should be recognizing?
- Is there anything keeping you from being successful in class?

- Recognize and reward students when they achieve learning targets, follow classroom rules, and apply classroom procedures.

- Harvest student wins by applying strategies that recognize specific performances and behaviors. Teachers need to see that their students will repeat those actions that are recognized and rewarded.

PRINCIPLE

Principle 5:
When Teachers Share Results, Everybody Wins

School leaders know that the best teachers at their schools determine what students know, identify where learning gaps are occurring, and create learning targets with measures that inform students and parents about what students need to do in order to hit the targets. Teachers may successfully create the targets and measures, but they are meaningless if teachers fail to explain the information to students so that they understand what is expected of them. When teachers also inform parents about the targets and measures, the parents can provide support to their children as they work toward the learning targets. School leaders should help teachers to successfully roll out learning targets, measures, and results every 30 days.

Great teachers constantly collect information on the measures they use to coach students. They measure and record 30-day learning targets and the aligned weekly targets. Teachers also share the final individual results with each of their students and the class results with all students. They set class goals for the learning targets to determine how well students achieved the measures. And at the end of a given 30-day period they provide the results.

Parents are important partners for teachers. That's why it is important for teachers to determine how satisfied parents are with their children's experiences in the classroom. At the end of 30 days, teachers should collect parent satisfaction data and roll out the results by sharing the data with parents.

In Chapter 13 we provide information school leaders need to know in order to help teachers analyze student and parent satisfaction results and ultimately determine which teaching methods are working and which ones need to be improved.

Sometimes teachers, like other professionals, will hide data they feel paint a negative picture of their classroom. However, we find that when teachers use data, share the results, and make changes based on the results, they are able to create better learning environments and both they and their students receive more "wins" in the classroom. Parents value being asked what they think, and they value being given student learning information about their children. Great teachers use data to harvest wins with students and parents, and in turn change good classrooms to great ones where everybody wins.

In compliance-driven classrooms, teachers judge how effective they are based on how they teach rather than how well their students learn. At the end of the year, teachers report to school leaders what they have covered in their class. They feel satisfied because they have taught what every student should learn.

On the other hand, teachers working in performance-driven classrooms focus on the actual results from two targeted groups, students and their parents. During the year teachers constantly determine how well students are hitting learning targets. They also gather and analyze information from parents to determine how satisfied they are with their children's learning experience. Equally important is the fact that teachers then share results with students and parents. They also use it to modify their teaching practices when needed.

In the next two chapters we describe what Tactics 13 and 14 look like when applied by teachers. Tactic 13 focuses on how teachers compile student learning and parent satisfaction data and use that data to improve the learning environment for students. Tactic 14 focuses on several strategies that teachers can use to reflect on their classroom practices and how teachers can constantly use student learning and parent satisfaction results to become better and better at their work.

Tactic 13:
Help Teachers Successfully Roll Out Data

Why Tactic 13 Is Important

School leaders know that instruction is the method teachers use to help students achieve learning targets. Teachers use different strategies, methods, and approaches when they are instructing students. Regardless of the instructional strategy used, teachers in performance-driven classrooms believe they have successfully taught their students only after they've seen evidence that their students have *learned* the material. The best teachers focus on what their students are learning rather than on their teaching methods.

One of the greatest teachers of our time, Coach Wooden, taught his basketball players how to execute the skills of their individual positions and how to play together as a team. He focused on what his players were learning and not learning. He then closed any learning gaps by teaching his players what they needed to do to improve. He watched and coached them as they practiced and measured their achievements as they learned. Coach Wooden took notes and used them to make decisions about what he could do to help his team improve. He also shared what he had learned from the information he gathered with players and coaches alike so that everyone was working from the same page.

When teachers execute 30-Day Plans, students know their 30-day learning targets and how those targets translate into weekly measures. When teachers create a way to provide daily feedback to students on their practice exercises and roll out summative test data, students see first-hand how they are doing and what they need to do to get closer to hitting the learning targets.

When teachers provide students with results data, they are better informed about their standing and are able to take control of their learning experience and make their own decisions about what they need to do to improve. When the goal in question is also a team or class goal, students will work with each other to achieve the goal. Some students will be the "starters" on the team while others will be the "back-ups." Teachers can interchangeably assign the "starter" or "back-up" role to students to give them opportunities to practice leading and supporting their classmates. When the starters are paired with their back-ups and both have a common goal, they will both have a chance to achieve the goal.

Think back to the story about Swen Nater. He was the "back-up" to Bill Walton. Both achieved great success in comparable positions in their lives. They helped each other become better centers on the basketball team. Likewise, when they work together in a similar fashion, students help each other achieve defined learning targets.

In addition to the teachers and students, the class team also includes a third member, the parents or caregivers of the students. When teachers help parents become part of the team rather than just spectators, they create a more supportive and open learning culture for the students. It is perfectly natural for parents to want to know how their children are doing in class. Keeping student results and other information from parents will only make them suspicious and anxious.

When teachers roll out aggregate class results to students at the end of each 30-day period, they can share the same data with parents. Doing so allows parents to see how well their own children performed on the learning targets in relation to the class average.

By seeing the results, parents learn where their children need additional help and support from them. They can also identify the exact learning targets and measures where their children are experiencing learning gaps. In other words, parents become partners with teachers and their children. When teachers share student learning information with parents every 30 days and make positive phone calls that follow the "three compliments to one criticism" principle, we find that parent satisfaction results increase.

As previously mentioned, in one of our programs we worked with 20 teachers, most of whom taught in high need schools, on how to properly prepare for the first 30 days of school. First, they learned the AIDET approach to help them with their calls with parents. They used AIDET in the calls they made to their students' parents prior to the beginning of the school year and also on the calls they made to them throughout the 30 days to give positive comments about their children. (Remember the "three compliments to one criticism" principle!) At the end of the time frame they sent home a brief parent survey asking parents how satisfied they were with their child's experience during the first 30 days of school.

The goal was for 70 percent of the parents to rate their satisfaction level with their child's experience a "5" out of a possible 5. The teachers experienced great success! After the completion of the first month of school, all 20 teachers met that goal.

At our meeting the day before pre-school began for teachers, one teacher, Ms. Gamble, commented on the significance of calling parents. She told her fellow teachers that in the 12 years of her daughter's and son's schooling she received only one introductory phone call from a teacher welcoming her and her child to the school year. Ms. Gamble said that she would never forget what that teacher had done to ensure the school year started on a positive note. She said her child's teacher was a star. She made a difference in the life of Ms. Gamble and her child and probably many others. Don't underestimate the difference one phone call can make for students and their parents.

We recommend that teachers give parents an option to provide input about their satisfaction with their children's experience. Tactic 13 provides a strategy for rolling out student learning and parent satisfaction results. The strategy keeps teachers, students, and parents focused on how well students are learning rather than on what the teacher is teaching.

Remember that as teachers begin to apply the tactics presented in the book, parent satisfaction results should get better and better. Administering classroom surveys to parents gives teachers opportunities to harvest wins with students and parents. Asking parents what they think encourages them to buy into their children's education. The results also provide opportunities for school leaders to reward and recognize student and teacher performance.

How to Apply Tactic 13

At the end of every 30 days, teachers must assess their students' learning results. The results consist of several summative assessments and a final assessment of the 30-day learning target. In addition, teachers should gather parent satisfaction data by asking them to complete a brief survey about their experience during a given 30-day period. Teachers then have the opportunity to roll out the results in three ways:

- Share individual student learning results with students and their parents
- Explain class results to students and their parents
- Share collective parent satisfaction results with parents

Individual Student Learning Results

Recall the team of sixth grade math teachers that was introduced in Chapter 9. That team of teachers created and implemented a 30-Day Plan and recorded their student learning and student behavior data into a spreadsheet. When the data are compiled in this way, teachers can use it to provide students and parents with 30-day results reports, similar to a quarterly earnings report that a business might send out to shareholders.

Figure 13.1 provides an example of a 30-day report one of the sixth grade math teachers created for a student in his class. Based on the report, the student and his parents can clearly see what was expected of him during the 30 days. They can also see how well he performed with regard to the state standard and each of its corresponding learning targets.

Figure 13.1. 30-Day Student Learning Results

Student Name:		
30-Day Student Learning Results		
30-Day State Standard/Benchmark: Develop an understanding of and fluency with multiplication and division of fractions.		
30-Day Learning Test Score		66 out of 70
30-Day Lesson Learning Target Scores Total		31 out of 40
• Simplify fractions.	7 out of 10	
• Multiply fractions and give answers in simplest fractions.	8 out of 10	
• Divide fractions and give answers in simplest fractions.	9 out of 10	
• Solve a word problem by multiplying and dividing fractions.	7 out of 10	
Total Possible Points		97 out of 110
Approximate Letter Grade to Date		B to A
30-Day Student Behavior		3 warnings
• 1st level warning	1	
• 2nd level warning	2	
• 3rd level warning	0	
• 4th level warning	0	
• 5th level warning	0	
Overall Behavior Assessment		Needs Improvement

© Janet K. Pilcher

The 30-day student learning results provide the standard/benchmark for the 30-Day Plan, the 30-day final test score, the scores for the four weekly learning targets that were assessed each week, the total points received out of the total possible, and the approximate letter grade for the 30-day period. The report also includes 30-day student behavior information with an overall assessment from the teacher. Possibilities include "Excellent," "Needs Improvement," and "Unacceptable." The teacher assessed that this student "Needs Improvement."

The report serves as an easy yet informative way for teachers to show students and their parents exactly where they stand at the end of a 30-day period. After seeing the reports students and parents can adjust behaviors or increase the focus on learning in order to make the next 30 days even better.

Class Student Learning Results

Figure 13.2 provides an example of how teachers can roll out student results for weekly learning targets and for the 30-day learning target. The maximum achievement level for the learning targets was 100 percent. As you can see, the only class goal not met was the learning target associated with word problems.

A teacher uses the detailed information in this spreadsheet to determine how many of his students continue to struggle with a particular learning target. If he determines that the number of struggling students is significant enough, he can decide to re-teach the topic and/or spend more time practicing the target. If he determines that only a few of the students are struggling, he can decide to team up one of the students who is doing well with the group that is struggling.

Once the struggling students have had more practice, the teacher reassesses the learning target and determines if the class is meeting the class goal. At the end of the 30 days, if the learning targets have been met, teachers and students can be recognized and rewarded at their 30-day celebration event. Always keep in mind that teachers will get more of those behaviors that are rewarded and recognized.

Figure 13.2. Roll Out of Class Data on Student Results

Learning Target from 30-Day Plan	Class Goals	Achievement Level
Given a fraction, apply the use of the GCF to simplify the fraction.	100% B or better	100%
Given a problem, solve by multiplying and giving the answer in the simplest fraction.	90% B or better	92%
Given a problem, solve by dividing and giving the answer in the simplest fraction.	90% B or better	90%
Given a word problem, solve by multiplying or dividing fractions.	80% B or better	78%
Given a number or word problem, solve by multiplying or dividing and giving the answer in the simplest fraction.	80% B or better	81%

© Janet K. Pilcher

Parent Satisfaction Results

At the beginning of each 30-day period, teachers should share the 30-day learning targets and overall goals and measures with parents. They should also inform parents that they will be providing them with an opportunity to give feedback at the end of the 30-day period. An example of a brief three-question parent satisfaction survey is provided in Figure 13.3. As you can see, parents are asked to rate how they feel about the following prompts on a scale of 1-5, with 5 being "strongly agree" and 1 being "strongly disagree":

1. Overall, I am satisfied with my child's experience in Ms. _____'s class.
2. I believe my child is learning.
3. I am clear about what my child is learning.

Figure 13.3. Sample 30-Day Parent/Caregiver Survey

Parent or Caregiver 30-Day Survey					
Dear _____, Thank you for taking time to complete the 30-day survey about _____'s learning experience in our class. I really value your input and your being a partner in _____'s learning. Sincerely, _____					
	Strongly Agree	Agree	Neutral	Disagree	Strongly Disagree
Overall, I am satisfied with my child's experience in Ms. _____'s class.	5	4	3	2	1
I believe my child is learning.	5	4	3	2	1
I am clear about what my child is learning.	5	4	3	2	1

© Janet K. Pilcher

When analyzing the survey information, teachers can assess surveys based on the average rating given for each question, the percentage of responses for each question by category, or the number of responses by each category for the three questions.

When using patient satisfaction surveys with healthcare organizations, Studer found that the most successful organizations receive at least 75 percent of their responses at level 5. He stresses that it is more important to determine what we need to do to move 4s to 5s rather than to focus on the very few 1s or 2s received.

For example, if about 70 percent of your parents rate prompt one at a "4," 25 percent a "5," and 5 percent at the other three levels, your goal should be to move the 70 percent of 4s to 5s. When parents rate their overall satisfaction at level "5," they are confident that their child is receiving a great education. Teachers use the scores from the other two survey items to determine if parents think their child is learning and if they think the learning expectations are clear.

Figure 13.4 provides a chart that maps the 30-day satisfaction scores of parents. The teacher wants 80 percent of the parents to provide an overall score of "5" on item one. Every 30 days, she records the 30-day survey ratings, shares the results with parents, and continues networking with parents to improve the satisfaction level with their children's learning experiences.

Most parents are not accustomed to being asked if they are satisfied with their children's educational experience. Therefore, teachers must work to build up trust in the parents that they are using the data in meaningful ways. The best way to do that is by rolling out the data and by making them partners in their children's learning.

Figure 13.4. Roll Out of Parent Satisfaction Data

	Goal	First 30 Days	Second 30 Days	Third 30 Days
Overall satisfaction with child's experience in class	80% score 5	72%	78%	82%

© Janet K. Pilcher

School leaders must help teachers successfully roll out student learning results and parent satisfaction data every 30 days. Doing so allows all involved—school leaders, teachers, students, and parents—to get a snapshot of how well students are learning and how satisfied parents are with the education their children are receiving.

Sharing the data with students provides them with a way to take control of their own learning and to determine what they need to do to improve in two areas, student learning and student behavior. Sharing the data with parents allows them to see how well their children have learned and how well their children have managed their behavior in class. After reviewing the data, teachers and parents can work together to help students manage their behavior, improve student learning, and recognize and reward success.

14

Tactic 14:
Help Teachers Use Data to Reflect Student Progress

Why Tactic 14 Is Important

In performance-driven classrooms, teachers constantly reflect on how well their students are learning. Teachers know that their success should be measured by how well their students have learned rather than how well they think they have taught. Many of the tactics in this book provide ways for teachers to collect and analyze information about student learning. These data help teachers know if and when they need to re-teach the content, provide more practice, and coach more.

When reflecting on a 30-day teaching period, teachers should use student learning and parent satisfaction results to shape their teaching practices for the next 30 days. To enhance their reflective practices, teachers can serve as coaches to each other. When they engage in focused conversations about their strategies for reinforcing student learning in their classrooms, teachers can learn from each other. These types of conversations are great ways for teachers to learn about teaching strategies that they otherwise may not have considered.

Tactic 14 focuses on how teachers can network with one another to discuss what teaching strategies are helping students hit their learning targets and what else they could be doing to further coach their students.

As part of this tactic, we recommend that school leaders create teacher learning teams that help individual teachers improve their self-reflection strategies and help the group as a whole reflect on and improve their teaching practices. The learning teams should be led by collegial coaches, teachers who serve the role of helping the teacher learning teams learn, plan, analyze, and reflect together, and include what we call "coaching probes."

When teacher learning teams are used, we find that teachers have an opportunity to think outside of their individual reflections and engage in dialogue with their colleagues that can help them improve their practices. Consequently, they also feel more confident about their abilities to manage their classrooms in ways that reinforce student learning. Collegial coaches help teachers reflect on their practices without judging or evaluating teacher behaviors.

Sometimes individuals use the terms *mentor* and *coach* interchangeably. Similar to Harry Wong, we argue that the two are quite different. To keep from getting confused, review Figure 14.1, which provides a breakdown of the differences between coaches and mentors. The chart, which was created by Wong, is taken from a February 2008 edition of the www.teachers.net newsletter. Wong provides five major purposes that we recommend coaches follow.

Figure 14.1. Description of Differences Between Mentors and Coaches

Differences Between Mentors and Coaches	
Mentors	Coaches
Are available for survival and support	Help teachers improve student learning
Provide emotional support and answer singular procedural questions	Coach to improve instructional skills on a sustained basis
React to whatever arises	Focus on student learning goals
Treat mentoring as an isolated activity	Participate as part of the job-embedded staff development process
Serve as just a buddy	Have leadership responsibilities

© Harry K. Wong

For Tactic 14, we recommend that teachers get together in teacher learning teams in order to reflect on their practices as they review 30-day student learning and parent satisfaction results.

In our own research, we are beginning to work more and more with collegial coaches and teacher learning teams. We are researching what methodologies work well—such as implementing the 30-day student learning period, involving parents in the education process, and reviewing teacher satisfaction results—as well as what methodologies need to be changed. So far the work that teachers have done in these teams has produced great results. A summary of the results is provided in Appendix 2.

How to Apply Tactic 14

Naturally, different teachers reflect on their practices in different ways. Teacher learning teams may not be for all teachers, but our research shows most find them to be beneficial. In addition to helping teachers improve student learning and parent satisfaction results in their classrooms, the teachers themselves rate their experience with the team and coach at a very high level.

Coaching Probes

The collegial coach of the teacher teams can be someone in the school or someone at another school. Alternately, the role can rotate from team member to team member in the teacher learning teams. Regardless, the teams work together to create individual or team 30-Day Plans.

As they implement the plans, the collegial coach completes what we call "coaching probes" with the team members by selecting a time during the 30 days to observe a block of instruction for each teacher on the team. Prior to the visit, the coach meets with the teacher to discuss the lesson being taught. The collegial coach uses the Coaching Probe Tool (Figure 14.2) to collect information during the visit. This tool specifically addresses how the teacher communicated the learning targets to students, how the instruction was aligned to the targets, how students received feedback on the targets, how students were engaged, and how well students understood classroom procedures.

Figure 14.2. Coaching Probe Tool

Coaching Probe Tool	
Probes	**Notes**
Do you see the learning targets written on the board? Describe.	
Do you see evidence of instruction aligned to the learning targets? Describe.	
Do you see students receiving feedback in class on the learning targets? Describe.	
Do students look like they are taking control of their learning? Describe.	
Do students seem to understand the classroom procedures? Describe.	

© Janet K. Pilcher

We previously mentioned that rounding serves a different purpose from that of classroom walk-throughs. "Coaching probes" are also different from classroom walk-throughs. The purpose of coaching probes is for teachers to coach each other on how they can help their students improve their learning.

Based on our experience with teacher learning teams, we recommend that the teacher serving as coach spend at least 45 minutes in a learning situation and try to schedule a time when she will get to see a unit of instruction begin and end for a given day. When the coach is in the classroom surveying the landscape, she records evidence using the Coaching Probe Tool in Figure 14.2.

At the end of the 30 days, the collegial coach meets with the team to reflect on the previous 30 days. They discuss the student learning and parent satisfaction results, which were rolled out from the 30-Day Plans, and they present the information they collected using the Coaching Probe Tool. At the team meeting, the teachers and the coach discuss their reflections based on the following four questions:

- What worked well?
- What challenges did I face?

- What modifications would I make to the lesson?
- Is there anything I need to learn, re-learn, or receive more practice on?

The results and the reflections guide the teachers on what they need to do to improve during the next 30 days and help the school leader know what he needs to do to support teachers to achieve their goals.

Rounding

The collegial coaches also use various strategies to harvest wins with teachers and to share those wins with their school leaders. The coaches round on the teachers once or twice a month. When rounding they ask the following questions:

- What is working well today?
- Are there any individuals I should be recognizing?
- Do you have the tools and equipment you need to do your job?
- Is there anything that we could improve?

The collegial coach records the information and sends a scouting report to the school leader. The school leader should create a system for following up on the items listed on the scouting report. The school leader, the coach, or any team member may elect to recognize teachers by using reward and recognition strategies such as sending thank-you notes, completing WOW cards, and acknowledging a colleague's great performance at meetings.

Bright Ideas

The coaching probes and rounding sessions provide ways for school leaders to harvest intellectual capital from teachers. Through our research in high need schools, we've found that the use of collegial coaches and coaching probe questions is an effective strategy for improving student learning results and increasing teacher satisfaction. The shared information also opens doors for school leaders to capture this same intellectual capital at their schools.

Studer created a strategy for harvesting intellectual capital in organizations. Modifying his strategy slightly, we recommend that teachers contribute "bright ideas" based on what they've discussed in their teacher learning teams.

Here's how it works: School leaders create a "Bright Idea" basket that is placed near their office. The teams complete a bright idea card (Figure 14.3) and place the card in the box. The leader establishes a review process to determine which bright ideas are doable in the school. For example, if the idea cannot work because of costs, the leader will need to put closure to the idea or make suggestions to the team on how to revise the idea in order to make it work. The team could then revise their bright idea and resubmit it.

When a school leader sees bright ideas that seem feasible and promising, the leader sends the "bright idea" card to a team of teachers. The team, established by the school leader, reviews the idea and makes a recommendation to the school leader, who then shares that information with the teacher learning team that submitted the bright idea. Either way the school leader should always give a response to the team, regardless of whether it is positive or negative.

We suggest that school leaders keep tracking charts of the bright ideas submitted, the team that submitted an idea, the date, and the action taken. Naturally, school leaders should implement the process that works best for them and their school. No matter the strategy used, school leaders must make sure they clearly communicate the process the school uses to gather, review, and act on "bright ideas."

Figure 14.3. Bright Idea Card

Bright Idea
Name: _____
School: _____
Date: _____
IDEA:
Please submit to the Bright Idea box....Thank you for sharing your idea!

Adapted with permission from Studer Group, 2001 ©

Teachers learn, grow, create, and perform better when they engage with other teachers who are also constantly striving to become better and better at what they do. Teachers within learning teams energize each other. They also help each other think about ways to improve that they might otherwise have missed.

Teachers improve when they reflect on what works and what does not work. When teachers share their reflections in their learning teams and have opportunities to study their peers' teaching strategies, all of the teachers involved learn and grow in their profession. Tactic 14 helps teachers work to become great in their work and to sustain greatness in their classrooms. And those teachers who act as collegial coaches help their peers become and remain great teachers.

Tactics 13-14:
When Teachers Share Results, Everybody Wins

To achieve student learning and parent satisfaction results, school leaders must coach and support teachers to:

- Know that student learning results must be transparent to students and their parents.

- Partner with parents and evaluate parent satisfaction levels. Then gather parent satisfaction data from parents at the end of every 30 days and share the collective results with them.

- Analyze student learning results to determine what is working and what is not working in their classrooms.

- Realize that rolling out data and making those results transparent gives teachers an opportunity to modify their practices and to harvest wins with parents and students. Teachers also realize that they get wins when students learn and when parents are satisfied with their children's learning experience. Teachers share results in three ways:

- Individual student learning results with students and their parents
- Class results with students and their parents
- Collective parent satisfaction results with parents

- Work in teacher learning teams. A team includes a collegial coach, who is one of their teacher colleagues in or outside of their school. The collegial coach uses the Coaching Probe Tool to observe a teacher's classroom and then discusses the observations at the 30-day team meeting. The five questions on the Coaching Probe Tool are:

  - Do you see the learning targets written on the board? Describe.
  - Do you see evidence of instruction aligned to the learning targets? Describe.
  - Do you see students receiving feedback in class on the learning targets? Describe.
  - Do students look like they are taking control of their learning? Describe.
  - Do students seem to understand the classroom procedures? Describe.

- Meet with teacher learning teams at the end of 30 days to talk about the data that are rolled out from the 30-Day Plan and their answers to the following four questions:

  - What worked well?
  - What challenges did I face?
  - What modifications would I make to the lesson?
  - Is there anything I need to learn, re-learn, or receive more practice on?

- Round for outcomes with each other and harvest intellectual capital by creating a system to share bright ideas.

Final Thoughts:
Connecting This Book's Tactics to Evidence from Business, Healthcare, and Education

Our goal with *How to Lead Teachers to Become Great: It's All About Student Learning* has been to transfer the leadership techniques developed by Jim Collins and Quint Studer for the business and healthcare worlds, respectively, to the education world. In it, we built off of their methods to create tactics that when implemented produce improved student learning and improved parent satisfaction results.

We focused so heavily on the teachings of Collins and Studer because their work in the world of leadership development is second to none. Collins uses his methodologies to show organizations how a focus on producing great leaders can take their performance from good to great. And Studer teaches the healthcare organizations he works with that a focus on producing great leaders can lead to results that last. Both of these authors reinforce that great leaders create organizational cultures that are results-driven and that run on consistency and coherence of goals, tactics, and measures.

Collins' and Studer's years of research and field experience show that it takes more than charisma to become a great leader. It takes hard work and dedication. They've found that great leaders intentionally create structures and processes that produce transparent results in their organizations—results that create passion in their employees and organizational cultures in which employees have purpose, do worthwhile work, and make a difference.

Both Collins and Studer use the concept of a flywheel in their methodology. The flywheel concept describes how businesses and organizations can move from a build-up process—the time in an organization where everyone is working to achieve specific goals—to breakthrough—the period when the goals have been achieved and the new goal becomes to sustain achievement and reach higher goals—in order to produce evidence-based results that are transparent to everyone—employees and customers alike.

In *How to Lead Teachers to Become Great*, we apply Studer's organizational flywheel, which he uses to create results-driven cultures in healthcare organizations, to classrooms. Using evidence-based leadership and evidence-based classroom learning frameworks, we explain how the organizational flywheel applies to school leaders as they coach and support teachers—the ultimate goal being to produce improved student learning and improved parent satisfaction results.

Organization Flywheel

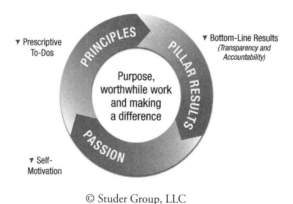

© Studer Group, LLC

The flywheel's hub is based on three important principles—purpose, worthwhile work, and making a difference. It reflects Studer's belief that nurses and doctors enter the healthcare profession because they want to make a difference in the lives of others. We feel the same can be said of teachers entering the education field.

The three spokes on the flywheel, when applied to classrooms, include tactics, results, and passion. In order to turn the flywheel, Studer teaches, leaders must put their prescriptive "to-dos" into action, which are connected to what he calls principles.

In this book, we describe five principles and 14 tactics associated with the prescriptive "to-dos" on the flywheel. When school leaders consistently and coherently apply the tactics, they are able to prioritize teacher support. These better-supported teachers garner improved student learning results, create parents who are satisfied with their children's learning experience, and re-ignite a passion for learning in students similar to the one they had on their very first day of school. Teachers, in turn, see that their work has purpose, is worthwhile, and makes a difference in their students' lives.

The tactics that make the flywheel spin for school leaders and teachers are derived from evidence-based classroom learning techniques based on several methodologies: Studer Group's evidence-based leadership in healthcare, the practices that Collins determined move companies from good to great and keep them there, several significant studies and practices in education, which link to decades of research, and our own experiences in education.

School leaders need to apply these tactics to recruit, select, coach, and support teachers in their efforts to be great at what they do every day in the classroom. The measures for applying the tactics are student learning and parent satisfaction results at each school.

When the flywheel spins, teachers shift from "hit and miss" student results in compliance-driven classrooms to student "results that last" in performance-driven classrooms. Unfortunately, students in compliance-driven classrooms fail to sustain learning gains because teachers must focus on what they *teach* instead of what students *learn*.

Performance-driven classrooms are supported by the Black and William study, which shows that students of teachers in these classrooms have higher standardized student achievement gains. The study findings indicate that the effect size was equal to a one standard deviation move up on standardized achievement tests—a remarkable increase.

However, students in performance-driven classrooms achieve "results that last" because teachers focus on what students are *learning*. Teachers communicate and demonstrate learning targets, let students practice, coach them as they are practicing, and assess them once they have had every opportunity to learn. When these tactics are consistently and coherently applied and school leaders provide the necessary support, the teachers who use them become great teachers. And great teachers produce great student learning results year after year.

The most effective school leaders know that teachers are the most important force affecting student learning. Therefore, accountability systems work well only when district and school accountability measurements directly connect to what teachers do with students and their parents. That's why in this book we focus on what school leaders need to do to coach and support teachers to become great.

A school leader's number one priority each day should be to help the teachers at his school achieve desired student learning results and to create a learning environment for students that is satisfactory to parents. Accountability for student learning specifically falls on the teacher. When goals are made to improve educational systems, the tactics used to reach those goals need to connect to what teachers do each day and provide teachers with the support that will allow them to do the best job possible.

The 14 tactics presented in this book do just that. They are supported by evidence-based leadership and evidence-based classroom learning frameworks, which provide the methodology needed to move teacher performance from good to great. The shift begins to occur when school leaders recognize that great schools are the result of the great teachers who teach in them. A school leader's priority must be to recruit, retain, coach, and support great teachers.

Rarely do leaders spend the time necessary to determine what it takes to build greatness. When school leaders elect to jump off of the latest district education bandwagon and instead start applying the tactics we've laid out in this book, their teachers have the opportunity to vastly improve, enjoy renewed purpose, feel more worthwhile, and realize the difference they make in the lives of every student they teach and every parent they contact.

How to Lead Teachers to Become Great covers tactics that empower school leaders across the country to help their teachers become great and in turn improve student learning results and parent satisfaction results. We hope readers will embrace these tactics by coaching and supporting their teachers as they learn to apply the tactics in their classrooms.

What we do as school leaders to support teachers influences the way teachers connect with their students. These tactics show leaders what they can and should expect from their teachers and what teachers can and should expect from them. Working together, we can all help students learn that they have purpose, can do worthwhile work, and make a difference in the lives of others and the world we live in.

Appendix 1:
Core Research and Principles Aligned with Evidence-Based Classroom Learning

In this book, we draw from what we consider some of the most significant works in education, business, and healthcare to date. These works include research results and the results of "tried and true" practices that have led to improved performance across several industries. By translating these findings into tactics that can be used in the classroom, we've outlined a methodology—evidenced-based classroom learning—which school leaders can use to recruit, retain, coach, and support great teachers.

In this book, we lay the foundation for evidence-based classroom learning. The references below in no way represent an exhaustive list of the many business and education experts who have influenced this book. Our work connects to the work of many others. However, these authors' contributions, along with our application of the tactics, provide the backbone for developing future research that will build on evidence-based classroom learning.

On the following pages we provide reference information for the publications and findings that most influenced us as we developed the 14 tactics outlined in *How to Lead Teachers to Become Great*:

1. **Black, Paul & Wiliam, Dylan (1998), Inside the Black Box: Raising Standards Through Classroom Assessment,** *Phi Delta Kappan,* **80(2), pp. 139-144.**

Paul Black and Dylan Wiliam were both professors at King's College London School of Education when they published *Inside the Black Box: Raising Standards Through Classroom Assessment.* Currently, Dylan Wiliam is Deputy Director of the Institute for Education, University of London, United Kingdom. He has also served as the Director of the Learning and Teaching Research Center at the Educational Testing Service. He has published over 150 articles, book chapters, and books in mathematics education, education law, and educational assessment. Wiliam is an international leader of research in exploring how classroom assessments support learning.

Paul Black is an emeritus professor of science education at King's College London and began his career as a faculty member in the Department of Physics in the University of Birmingham (England). His interests and research include formative and summative assessment and science curriculum in schools. Black has also been a visiting professor at Stanford University, California. He is currently engaged in research and development work to improve classroom practices in formative assessments.

Black and Wiliam coauthored the publication *Inside the Black Box: Raising Standards Through Classroom Assessment.* In it they present what we consider to be some of the most significant findings in education on student learning. Their study focuses on one particular aspect of teaching, formative assessment, which occurs in classrooms. Their findings show that teachers who use formative assessments and who provide consistent feedback are more effective at increasing student learning results. Black and Wiliam conducted an extensive survey of the books and journals on this topic over a nine-year time period. That survey of materials yielded about 580 articles or chapters that focused on formative classroom assessment and feedback practices by teachers. Of the 580 manuscripts, they selected 250 to review. They found that teachers who used formative assessment practices in their classrooms significantly improved their students' performance on standardized tests. The highest gains occurred for lower performing students.

2. Bloom, B. (1956). *Taxonomy of Educational Objectives: The Classification of Educational Goals, Handbook 1: Cognitive Domain.* **New York: Longmans, Green.**

About 50 years ago, Bloom wrote this handbook to create a common language about learning goals. To do so, he presented five hierarchical learning domains with capability verbs linked to each domain. The learning and capability verb domains serve as the basis for creating performance objectives that are used to develop standardized tests and measures. Bloom promoted using the domains to create aligned learning objectives, learning activities, and assessments in courses and curricula.

3. Brooks, D. (1985). "The First Days of School." *Educational Leadership,* **May 1986, pp. 76-79.**

On the first page of Chapter 1 in *The First Days of School: How to Be an Effective Teacher*, Harry and Rosemary Wong cite the research Douglas Brooks presents in his article "The First Days of School." While observing a group of teachers, Brooks found that those who started the first day of school with a fun activity spent the rest of the school year struggling to manage negative student behavior in their classrooms. Teachers who started by emphasizing good organization and outlining classroom procedures effectively managed students and created an environment where students had opportunities for learning.

4. Collins, Jim (2001). *Good to Great: Why Some Companies Make the Leap...and Others Don't.* **New York, NY: HarperCollins, Publishers.**

Jim Collins has compiled a decade of research on how great companies grow, attain superior performance, become great, and sustain greatness. Collins began his teaching career as a faculty member at Stanford Graduate School of Business. In 1995 he founded a management laboratory in Boulder, Colorado, where he conducts research and teaches corporate executives from the public and private sectors. He complemented his book *Good to Great* by writing a monograph, *Good to Great and the Social Sectors.*

Jim Collins begins his book with this sentence, "Good is the enemy of great." As research for his book, he and a team of researchers studied a group of companies for five years to determine how good companies could become great. The team started with about 1,500 companies and used a data analysis strategy to identify 11 companies that made the breakthrough to greatness. They found that companies that moved from "good" to "great" had a history of cumulative stock returns equal to or below the general stock market. Those returns were then followed by a breakthrough that led to performance with cumulative returns of at least three times the general market for 15 years following their breakthrough point. Jim Collins and his research team created a framework to describe good to great companies. All of the principles of the framework were evident 100 percent of the time in "good to great" companies, and 30 percent or less were evident in comparison companies. In his monograph, Collins took what he learned from great companies and applied the same principles to the social sectors.

5. **Downey, C., Steffy, B., English, F., Frase, L. & Poston, W. (2004).** *The Three-Minute Classroom Walk-Through: Changing School Supervisory Practice One Teacher at a Time.* **SAGE Publications.**

This book introduces the Downey Walk-Through Method, which was developed 40 years ago and has been tested and refined in teachers' classrooms over the 40-year period. Carol Downey and her colleagues designed a three-minute walk-through for school leaders to use in teachers' classrooms. During the walk-through, school leaders focused on answering five questions. In this book, we used the concept of the walk-through questions to create the coaching probes for the teacher learning teams.

6. **Fuller, B., Hannum, E. & Henne, M. (2008).** *Strong States, Weak Schools: The Benefits and Dilemmas of Centralized Accountability.* **Bingley, UK: Emerald Group Publishing, Ltd.**

This recent report, supported by the RAND Corporation, proposes that school and district policies have a relatively weak influence on teachers' classroom instruction. When trying to improve their schools, rather than help their teachers improve through professional development and outcome goals, school leaders spend their time trying to change something in the system. Consequently, teachers' classrooms are relatively autonomous with little uniformity in applying best practices that yield student learning results. We use this report to develop a rationale for designing tactics that directly affect student learning results.

7. **Nater, Swen & Gallimore, Ronald (2006).** *You Haven't Taught Until They Have Learned: John Wooden's Teaching Principles and Practices.* **Morgantown, WV: Fitness Information Technology.**

In the foreword of the book Bill Walton writes, "Swen Nater's story is really one of the greatest stories ever told. It would be difficult to make up a more unlikely story than Swen's rise to glory both on and off the basketball court. And his success is due in large part to the teaching methods of Coach Wooden, which are detailed in *You Haven't Taught Until They Have Learned.*" He goes on to say that in the book Nater and Gallimore perfectly capture why Coach Wooden's success has influenced so many people in so many walks of life.

We include examples of Coach Wooden's teaching practices because we believe he is truly one of the greatest teachers of all time. Nater, one of his players and students, applied what he learned from Coach Wooden to become a great basketball player, a great teacher and coach, and a great contributor to others. Coach Wooden is a difference-maker and lives his life teaching others how to make differences in the lives of those they touch. Though he may not have called them the same thing, Coach Wooden practiced some of the tactics outlined in this book long before we put them down on paper.

8. **Marzano, R., Marzano, J. & Pickering, D. (2003).** *Classroom Management That Works: Research-Based Strategies for Every Teacher.* **Association for Supervision and Curriculum Development.**

Similar to the research method Black and Wiliam used when studying the formative classroom assessment strategies of teachers, Bob Marzano and colleagues conducted a meta-analysis to synthesize the research on effective schools. He and his colleagues analyzed research studies that had been conducted over a 35-year span. Marzano separated the effect of a school on student achievement from the effect of an individual teacher on student achievement. The summary of results is extremely revealing and provides strong support for the idea that teachers are the most important variable affecting student learning. Their results revealed:

- A student at the 50th percentile who attends an average school and has an average teacher achieves at the 50th percentile at the end of two years.

- The same student at the 50th percentile who attends a least effective school and has an ineffective teacher drops to the 3rd percentile at the end of two years.

- The same student at the 50th percentile who attends a highly effective school and has an ineffective teacher achieves at the 37th percentile at the end of two years.

- The same student at the 50th percentile who attends a highly effective school and has a highly effective teacher achieves at the 96th percentile at the end of two years.

- The same student at the 50th percentile who attends a least effective school and has a highly effective teacher achieves at the 63rd percentile at the end of two years.

This last scenario shows how important an individual teacher is to student learning. As Marzano states, "Even if the school they work in is highly ineffective, individual teachers can produce powerful student learning gains."

9. **Pilcher, J., Largue, R. & Ellis, H. (2007).** *Aligning Instruction to Standards: Just Ask Andie.* **Pensacola, FL: Institute for Innovative Community Learning.**

The Lesson Architect® is a free online tool for teachers that helps them align their instruction to state standards. *Aligning Instruction to Standards* is a guide that provides instruction on standards alignment and complements the online tool. It uses a "tell me, show me, and guide me" format. The online tool and guide use sound assessment processes as the centerpiece for designing good instruction. Pilcher and Largue use both the tool and the guide to prepare new and "soon-to-be" teachers in two highly successful programs. These two resources as well as many others can be found at www.teacher-ready.net.

10. **Snow, C., Barnes, W., Chandler, J., Goodman, I., & Hemphill, L. (2000).** *Unfulfilled Expectations: Home and School Influences on Literacy.* **Authorhouse, Inc.**

Catherine Snow is the Henry Lee Shattuck Professor of Education at the Harvard Graduate School of Education. Her research interests include "children's language development as influenced by interaction with adults in home and preschool settings, literacy development as related to language skills and as influenced by home and school factors, and issues related to the acquisition of English oral and literacy skills by language minority children." With a team of researchers, she coauthored *Unfulfilled Expectations: Home and*

School Influences on Literacy. The team focused on something very significant—home influences on student achievement.

In particular, they focused on the literacy achievement of elementary children from low income families. They studied the same 31 children for two years. Catherine Snow and the team focused on the effects of high and low levels of home and school support. They discovered some dramatic findings, which all educators should attune to when reviewing their practices.

- Students who had low home support and low classroom support had no chance of achieving successful literacy scores.

- Students who had high home support and low classroom support had a 60 percent chance of achieving successful literacy scores.

- Students who had mixed home support and mixed classroom support had a 25 percent chance of achieving successful literacy scores.

Three situations that are provided below represent students with a 100 percent chance to achieve successful literacy scores. The finding in the third bullet below reinforces that the teacher is the most important variable that affects student learning. These three situations are:

- Mixed classroom support and high home support;

- High classroom support and high home support; and

- High classroom support and low home support

Catherine Snow and Robert Marzano completed excellent studies and reported results that reinforce the relevance of effective teaching on student learning.

11. **Stiggins, R., Arter, J., Chappuis, S. & Chappuis, J., (2007).** *Classroom Assessment for Student Learning: Doing It Right—Using It Well.* **Educational Testing Services.**

Rick Stiggins is the founder and executive director of the Assessment Training Institute. Stiggins and his colleagues have focused on classroom assessment for about three decades. From his research, he has learned and now strongly promotes that teachers should engage students in the classroom assessment process. In our book, we integrate many suggestions from his work. Stiggins's research and work with teachers provides a substantial principle of the framework for evidence-based classroom learning. Below we provide several examples of publications that support the development of tactics focused on classroom assessment strategies.

- Stiggins, R. & Chappuis, J. (2008). Enhancing Student Learning. *The District Administrator,* January.

- Stiggins, R. (2007). Assessment Through the Student's Eyes. *Educational Leadership*, 67 (8), 22-26.

- Stiggins, R. & Chappuis, J. (2006). What a Difference a Word Makes: Assessment FOR Learning Rather Than Assessment OF Learning Helps Students Succeed. *Journal of Staff Development*, 27(1), 10-14.

- Stiggins, R. (2005). From Formative Assessment to Assessment FOR Learning: A Path to Success in Standards-Based Schools. *Phi Delta Kappan,* 87(4) December 2005, pp. 324-328.

- Chappuis, J. (2005). Helping Students Understand Assessment. *Educational Leadership,* 63(3), 39-43.

- Stiggins, R. & Chappuis, J. (2005). Using Student-Involved Classroom Assessment to Close Achievement Gaps. *Theory Into Practice,* 44(1), 11-18.

- Stiggins, R. (2001). The Unfulfilled Promise of Classroom Assessment. *Educational Measurement: Issues and Practice,* 20(3), 5-15.

- Stiggins, R. (1999). Assessment, Student Confidence, and School Success. *Phi Delta Kappan,* 81(3), 191-198.

- Stiggins, R., Frisbie, D., Griswold (1989). Inside High School Grading Practices: Building a Research Agenda. *Educational Measurement: Issues and Practices, 8,* 5-19.

12. **Studer, Q. (2008).** *Results That Last: Hardwiring Behaviors That Will Take Your Company to the Top.* **Hoboken, New Jersey, John Wiley & Sons.**

Studer, Q. (2004). *Hardwiring Excellence: Purpose, Worthwhile Work, Making a Difference.* **Pensacola, Florida, Fire Starter Publishing.**

Several years ago we read Quint Studer's first book, *Hardwiring Excellence,* which introduced us to the healthcare flywheel and showed examples of how employees in hospitals drastically improved their performance and the performance of the organization. We then heard Quint present at one of his *Taking You and Your Organization to the Next Level* sessions. At that time, we knew that the results he mastered as a manager and CEO in healthcare could be translated and hardwired into schools.

In particular, because of our work with pre-service and early career teachers, we saw great value in starting to put the strategies and tactics described in his recent bestseller, *Results That Last,* into action for school leaders and teachers. As we began working with teachers to apply several strategies from Studer's work and our work focusing on classroom assessment and management, we saw that the strategies were helping teachers improve their students' learning.

David F. Giannetto, coauthor of *The Performance Power Grid: The Proven Method to Create and Sustain Superior Organizational Performance*, praised Studer with these words, "I have always been fascinated by how the various parts of an organization work together to achieve strategic objectives. In *Results That Last*, Quint Studer explores the complex subject of performance improvement in a fresh, readable, and easy-to-grasp way."

We borrowed the principles and tactics from *Results That Last* to develop several of the 14 tactics. We too hope that *How to Lead Teachers to Become Great: It's All About Student Learning* is written in a "fresh, readable, and easy-to-grasp way."

Studer's accomplishments in the organizations he has led and coached are extraordinary. Named one of the "Top 100 Most Powerful People" by *Modern Healthcare*, he has gained national recognition (*USA Today, Inc. Magazine, Investor's Business Daily*) as a change agent and thought leader in healthcare today because he so aptly links a sustained focus on service, quality, employee and patient satisfaction with growth and bottom-line results.

Studer's first book, *Hardwiring Excellence*, was published in April 2004 and has since sold more than 300,000 copies. His second book, *101 Answers to Questions Leaders Ask*, was released in March 2005. Quint's third book, *Results That Last*, published by Wiley in fall 2007, shares the insights Studer has gained through a lifetime of experience. Thanks to Studer's excellent reputation, *Results That Last* became an Amazon.com bestseller even before it was published and once published became a *Wall Street Journal* bestseller. Studer also serves on the board of the Association of University Programs in Health Administration (AUPHA). AUPHA is the only non-profit entity of its kind that works to improve the delivery of health services throughout the world, and thus the health of citizens, by educating professional managers at the entry level.

With his early training in teaching (He received a B.A. degree in education and M.S. degree in education from University of Wisconsin, Whitewater), Studer's classroom is today one of the largest in health care. He and his team at Studer Group® coach more than 400 hospitals and health systems on their journey to becoming world-class leaders in service and operational excellence. Studer Group clients span the nation and include every type of healthcare organization (for-profit and not-for-profit), from small rural hospitals to some of the most-respected organizations and largest health systems. They include recipients of the prestigious Malcolm Baldrige National Quality Award.

Before founding Studer Group, Studer spent nearly 20 years inside healthcare, beginning in a staff position, later becoming COO of Holy Cross Hospital in Chicago and President of Baptist Hospital Inc. in Pensacola, Florida, where the hospital was awarded the Quality Cup by *USA Today* and Rochester Institute of Technology. At Holy Cross and Baptist, Studer led both organizations to the top one percent in employee and patient satisfaction compared to hospitals nationwide, as ranked by independent healthcare survey organizations.

13. **Wong, H. & Wong, R. (2004).** The First Days of School: How to Become an Effective Teacher. **Harry Wong Publications, Inc.**

Harry Wong is the most well-known and respected educator on classroom management in the nation. Through his books and his wonderful presentations, he has touched almost every teacher in some way. Over the past three decades the classroom management strategies that the Wongs recommend in their bestselling book have produced effective teachers in classrooms. Teachers using the strategies have reported that they have a zero dropout rate in classrooms, no discipline problems where classroom procedures are clearly defined, a 95 percent homework turn-in rate, and most of all, their students are learning. On www.teachers.net, Wong and his wife,

Rosemary, have captured thousands of examples from teachers of how their strategies have helped students learn.

Wong highly influences our work. We borrow from his successes and reinforce that creating and communicating classroom rules, their consequences, and classroom procedures serves as a cornerstone for teachers who strive to be effective in the classroom and who are dedicated to helping their students achieve results that last.

APPENDIX

Appendix 2:
Results from Teacher Learning Pilot Group Study

Over the past two years, we piloted the implementation of the 14 tactics covered in this book in several high need schools in the Escambia County School District in Pensacola, Florida. As part of one of our programs, we targeted 20 elementary school teachers in the district's highest need schools, which were labeled struggling schools. A breakdown of the demographics of each school is provided in Figure 1.

The feedback from the teachers who participated in this program provided us with invaluable insight into how best to further develop and implement the tactics.

We would like to thank all of the teachers who participated for the difference they make each day in the lives of their students. We would also like to thank the state of Florida Department of Education and the organization's bureau chief, Kathy Hebda, for supporting the teachers with grant funding for their professional development.

DEMOGRAPHICS OF PARTICIPATING ELEMENTARY SCHOOLS

Figure 1

	Semmes	Spencer Bibbs	Montclair	Warrington
School Grade for Past Five Years	01-D 02-D 03-C 04-D 05-F 06-F	01-D 02-D 03-C 04-D 05-D 06-D	01–C 02–C 03–C 04–D 05–D 06–F	01-C 02-C 03-C 04-C 05-D 06-C
% of Students on Free/Reduced Lunch	95.29%	97.8%	98%	87.6%
% of Minority Students	95%	97.8%	92%	64.2%
Teacher Turnover Rate for Past Five Years	01- 02- 03-15% 04-27% 05-27%	01- 02- 03-43% 04-20% 05-24%	01- 02- 03- 04- 05-	01- 02- 03-8.7% 04- 05-16%
# of Principals for Past Five Years	2	2	2	1

Summary of Results from the Pilot Group Study

Twenty teachers in high need schools in the Escambia County School District in Pensacola, Florida, completed a six-month teaching academy called the *Teachers Teach, Students Learn Academy* (TTSLA). The teachers worked in teams with an assigned coach, who was not a teacher at their school. The coaches attended all training events with the teachers, rounded on the teachers, guided the development of their 30-Day Plans (Chapter 8), completed a coaching probe with them in their classrooms (Chapter 14), and met with the team to reflect on what they had observed.

The teachers and coaches attended informational and training meetings with the group and their coach. Also, the coaches had one-on-one meetings with the teachers. They attended a week-long summer institute that focused on helping them become successful during the first 30 days of school, and they attended three day-long professional development sessions with education experts.

The Academy included content and opportunities for them to practice what they had learned on classroom rules and procedures, classroom assessments, and literacy. They also completed their 30-Day Plans following the format described in Chapter 8. Essentially, they created 30-day learning targets with aligned weekly targets and determined how they were going to assess student learning. The teachers then implemented their 30-Day Plans during the first month of school. During those 30 days, their coaches continued to round on them and also completed coaching probes using the Coaching Probe Tool, which is part of the coaching process described in Chapter 14. The teachers used the AIDET approach, described in Chapter 5 of this book, to connect with their students' parents and administered a parent survey at the end of the 30 days. Each teacher had two 30-day learning targets, one associated with classroom rules and procedures and a second that focused on developing a particular literacy skill, which varied by each team of teachers.

At the program's completion, we gathered data to determine student learning results, parent satisfaction results, and teacher satisfaction results. Read on for a summary of our findings.

Student Learning Results

Student results data, collected during the final assessment of the first 30 days, were reported by 18 of the 20 teachers. One non-reporting teacher did not have a class during the first 30 days. She rotated from class to class to assist students in various classrooms. The other non-reporting teacher was moved from one grade to another because of the decreased number of students in the grade she was teaching at the time. It is also important to note that about one-half of the participating teachers did not receive their district required classroom reading books and materials at the beginning of the school year and still had not received them at the end of their first 30 days.

When debriefing the 20 teachers, many commented that they spent a lot of time during the first 30 days teaching, re-teaching, and assessing classroom rules and procedures. They also spent a large portion of time diagnosing the learning capabilities of each of their students in order to create baseline measurements that could be used to develop and implement 30-Day Plans in various content areas. Naturally, students came into their classrooms at various learning levels.

After attending the Academy, they saw great value in beginning instruction at a student's learning level rather than at his or her "grade" level. The teachers stressed they spent valuable time during the first 30 days to gather data to determine each of their students' beginning learning point.

We believe that they were able to see the value in gaining an initial "good" measurement because they were focused on helping their students achieve the 30-day learning target. In other words, to get to the end, they had to know where to begin. The teachers' concentration on the 30-day learning target helped them focus on student learning rather than on what they were teaching.

Also, they assessed student performance with the classroom rules and procedures. They commented that regularly communicating, teaching, practicing, and assessing classroom rules and procedures afforded them a well-managed classroom. All teachers reported that they felt confident in their ability to manage their classrooms and reported that the professional development they received in the Academy helped them achieve better-managed classrooms.

They also reported results from the implementation of their 30-Day Plans. The teachers reported data on two questions.

1. Did your students hit your 30-day rules and procedures goal?
   - 100% of students in the teachers' classrooms achieved the goal

2. Did your students hit your 30-day literacy goal?
   - 100% of students achieved goal   6 teachers
   - 96% of students achieved goal   1 teacher
   - 80% of students achieved goal   1 teacher

- 70% to 75% of students achieved goal   3 teachers
- 60% to 67% of students achieved goal   7 teachers

Parent Satisfaction Results

Teachers used the AIDET approach to call their students' parents. They informed the parents that they would be sending a 30-day parent satisfaction survey to them to complete. The first 30-day results provided baseline data for teachers, as shown in Figure 2. We established a very challenging goal, which was for the teachers to receive the highest rating, a 4, for questions 1, 2, and 3 from 70 percent of the parents.

The teachers reported remarkable results. During the first 30 days, 70 percent of the parents responded with the highest rating for the first two questions and 68 percent for the third question. We believe that the AIDET approach and the 30-Day Plan helped teachers get these initial high marks.

Figure 2

	Strongly Disagree	Disagree	Agree	Strongly Agree
Overall, I am satisfied with my child's experience at school.		1	59	138
I believe that my child is learning this year.		2	57	138 (70%)
I feel comfortable with my child's teacher.	1	1	52	135 (68%)
So far, this is the best year my child has had in school.	1	4	75	114 (58%)

© Janet K. Pilcher

Teacher Satisfaction Results

Our goal was for at least 80 percent of the teachers to rate their experience in the Academy at the highest rating. We administered a survey at the end of the program and 100 percent of the teachers rated their experience a "5." At the end of six months, we asked the teachers to complete the survey in Figure 3 to rate their experience with the *Teachers Teach, Students Learn Academy*. We reached our goal with every question except one: "I have the materials and equipment to do the task right." We discovered from our debriefing discussions and the coaches' rounding feedback that some groups lacked the instructional literacy resources needed to carry out their 30-Day Plans.

Prior to the school year, the teachers received funds to create a classroom library, and the grant covered an instructional materials fee for the Academy materials. We elected to re-allocate some of the materials fee to purchase additional literacy resources, which aligned more with the learning level of the students in their classrooms. The need for these materials became clear to the teachers as they implemented their 30-Day Plans.

We discovered that teachers were more excited about receiving the materials for their classrooms than they were about receiving a stipend for their time in the Academy and their first 30 days of instruction. That said, we strongly believe that the small stipend the participating teachers received was well earned and well deserved for the worthwhile work they completed and the results they achieved.

The teachers responded to the survey questions below by selecting one of the ratings:

5   This aspect of the Academy is the best possible.

4   This aspect of the Academy is of high quality but could be better.

3   This aspect of the Academy is acceptable.

2   I am more dissatisfied than satisfied with this aspect of the Academy.

1   I am dissatisfied with this aspect of the Academy.

Figure 3

	1	2	3	4	5
I know what is expected of me in the Academy.					20 (100%)
I have all the materials and equipment to do the task right.				5	15 (75%)
I receive praise and recognition from my coach for good work.					20 (100%)
My principal recognizes and praises my good work.		1		3	16 (80%)
I receive feedback from my team members to help me improve my practices.			1	1	18 (90%)
In my team, my opinions seem to count.				4	16 (80%)
Belonging to the Academy makes me feel that my job is important.					20 (100%)
My team is committed to doing quality work.			1	1	18 (90%)
I learned something that will help me improve.					20 (100%)
I learned something that I can apply in my classroom.					20 (100%)
I believe that when I apply what I have learned I will improve student performance.					20 (100%)
The Academy was well organized.				1	19 (95%)
I would recommend the Academy to other teachers.					20 (100%)

Create great places for teachers to teach, students to learn, and parents to send their children.

Access the resources and tools highlighted in *How to Lead Teachers to Become Great* **and the resources listed below at www.studergroup.com/education. Some of these resources have been created for Studer Group healthcare partners, but they relate and can be adapted to fit your needs in the education arena.**

Speaking Engagements:

The coauthors, Janet Pilcher, Ph.D., and Robin Largue, Ed.D., are both available to speak. They have taken Evidence-Based Leadership[SM] tactics directly to the schoolhouse by applying them to what leaders can do to help teachers get better student learning results and ensure parents are satisfied with their children's experiences in school. Learn how to:

- Help school leaders recruit and retain highly effective teachers
- Provide techniques for dealing with low performing teachers
- Help leaders create a results-driven culture
- Guide teachers on what they can expect from leaders

- Focus teachers on what students are learning rather than what they, themselves, are teaching

The Institute for Innovative Community Learning® (ICL) is an entrepreneurial center at the University of West Florida dedicated to making a difference in education and in the community, and we bring the two together. Visit online programs, courses, just-in-time learning resources and tools, and online access to information:

TeacherReady® is the one-stop online learning place for "soon-to-be" and new teachers. Visit www.teacherready.net.

Just Ask Andie® provides great teacher "tidbits." These tidbits are snippets of good ideas with brief, but detailed, descriptions of how the ideas were implemented in a classroom. Find Andie at www.teacherready.net.

Studer Group Tools:

Rounding Tools available for download at www.studergroup.com/education:

- Leader Rounding on Employees Log
- Rounding on Staff Form
- Principal's Scouting Report
- Stoplight Report

Studer Group Books:

Results That Last by Quint Studer
In _Results That Last_, "Master of Business" Quint Studer shows you how to build an organizational culture that develops great leaders today and instills the mechanisms and the mindset that will continue to foster great leadership tomorrow. Studer presents the most effective leadership practices and shows

you how to apply them across every group, department, or division, resulting in improved leadership and performance on the individual, group, and organizational levels.

Hardwiring Excellence by Quint Studer
A bestseller that helps healthcare professionals rekindle the flame and offers a road map to creating and sustaining a Culture of Service and Operational Excellence that drives bottom-line results.

Studer Group Training Videos:

highmiddlelow® Performer Conversations
A video series for improving employee performance.

Selecting Talent Self-Instructional DVD Package
Train your leaders on the core leadership competency of selecting and retaining high performing staff.

AIDET^{SM} Five Fundamentals of Patient Communication
AIDET—Acknowledge, Introduce, Duration, Explanation, and Thank You—is a powerful communication tool.

Studer Group Webinars:

Conducting highmiddlelow Performer Conversations
Are low performers sucking the life out of your organization? Do you lie awake at night dreading the coaching conversations you need to have with people who aren't meeting expectations?

Leading Effective Meetings
Leaders report that as much as 33 percent of their time is spent in meetings and up to 50 percent of meeting time is unproductive!

Selecting Talent—Peer Interviewing Works!
The only thing worse than a good hire who leaves is a bad hire who stays. Learn how to avoid disastrous hires that drag down performance.

Time and Energy Management
Organizations that support work-life blend will have happier, healthier staff when they provide the tools employees need to take control of their personal goals for work-life blend.

Studer Group Institutes:

Taking You and Your Organization to the Next Level with Quint Studer
Learn the tools, tactics, and strategies that are needed to Take You and Your Organization to the Next Level at this two-day institute with Quint Studer and Studer Group's Coach Experts. You will walk away with your passion ignited and with Evidence-Based Leadership strategies to create a sustainable culture of excellence.

About Studer Group:

Studer Group's mission is to change the face of healthcare by creating a better place for employees to work, physicians to practice medicine, and patients to receive care. Studer Group is an outcomes-based healthcare performance improvement firm that coaches hundreds of hospitals, health systems, medical practices, and end-of life organizations to achieve and sustain clinical results. To learn more about Studer Group, visit www.studergroup.com.

ACKNOWLEDGMENTS

After reading *Hardwiring Excellence* and attending Quint Studer's *Taking You and Your Organization to the Next Level* presentations, we began developing and piloting tactics that are based on his body of work. Studer's influence and devotion to results-driven environments motivated us to apply the tactics to teachers and school leaders. From day one, our goal has been to help them improve their performance and that of their students. The results of this new style of teacher training have been gratifying to everyone: the teachers themselves, the students (who responded beautifully to the use of established learning goals), and their delighted parents.

We write this book with deep gratitude to Quint for his support and his constant belief that we could and can provide school leaders, teachers, and parents with a platform that allows them to have a purpose, feel worthwhile, and make a difference in the lives of young people.

Thank you, Quint, for making a difference in our lives so that we could make a difference in the lives of teachers and their students.

We would also like to thank our good friend Dr. Theresa Vernetsen for reading, editing, and listening to our ideas. We have relied on her expertise, advice, and many years of invaluable experiences in education. She is a valued and true friend to us and to our field.

Many thanks go to all the new teachers we have worked with in the TeacherReady® program and the *Teachers Teach, Students Learn Academy*. You are the difference makers for our young people, and you make our work have purpose.

Janet Pilcher, Ph.D., is a professor at the University of West Florida and is director of the school's Institute for Innovative Community Learning® (ICL), the entrepreneurial center she created. She has also served as the Dean of the College of Professional Studies, where she led several departments, including education; social work; criminal justice and legal studies; health, leisure, and exercise science; and engineering and computer technology. Janet has a bachelor's degree in marketing from Florida State University, a master's degree in educational leadership from the University of West Florida, and a Ph.D. from Florida State University in measurement and evaluation.

Robin Largue, Ed.D., has more than 30 years of experience as a district leader, high school principal, teacher, and educational leadership faculty member. At the University of West Florida she served as coordinator of the Educational Leadership Program and is now the chief instruction officer at the Institute for Innovative Community Learning® (ICL). Robin has a bachelor's degree from the University of Alabama in history education, a master's degree in history from the University of West Florida, and an educational doctorate degree in leadership and higher education from Florida State University.

INDEX

How to Order Additional Copies of

How to Lead Teachers to Become Great

Orders may be placed:
Online at:
www.firestarterpublishing.com
www.studergroup.com

By phone at: 866-354-3473

By mail at: Fire Starter Publishing
913 Gulf Breeze Parkway, Suite 6
Gulf Breeze, FL 32561

(Bulk discounts are available.)

How to Lead Teachers to Become Great
is also available online at www.amazon.com.